THE COLUMBIA ANTHOLOGY OF TRADITIONAL KOREAN POETRY

TRANSLATIONS FROM THE ASIAN CLASSICS

THE COLUMBIA ANTHOLOGY OF TRADITIONAL KOREAN POETRY

Edited by Peter H. Lee

COLUMBIA UNIVERSITY PRESS   NEW YORK

THIS BOOK IS PUBLISHED WITH THE SUPPORT OF
THE KOREA LITERATURE TRANSLATION INSTITUTE.

 Columbia University Press
Publishers Since 1893
New York   Chichester, West Sussex

Library of Congress Cataloging-in-Publication Data

The Columbia anthology of traditional Korean poetry / edited by Peter H.
Lee.
        p. cm. — (Translations from the Asian classics)
    ISBN 978-0-231-11112-6 (cloth : alk. paper)
    ISBN 978-0-231-11113-3 (pbk. : alk. paper)
    1. Korean poetry—To 1900—Translations into English.   I. Lee,
Peter H., 1929– II. Series.

    PL984.E3 C65 2002
    895.7′1008—dc21   2002067459

Printed in the United States of America

for Samantha, her parents, and her uncle and aunt

CONTENTS

SIJO   *69*

POETRY IN CHINESE   *201*

FOLK SONGS   *263*

SHAMANIST NARRATIVE SONGS   *281*

PREFACE

The year 1997 saw the publication of the five-volume Korean literature library edited by five scholars at Seoul National University. The first volume, on classical poetry, was compiled by Kwŏn Tuhwan; the second, on classical fiction, by Yi Sangt'aek; and the third, on oral literature, by Sŏ Taesŏk. The fourth and fifth volumes, on modern poetry and fiction, were compiled by O Seyŏng and David McCann and Kwŏn Yŏngmin and Bruce Fulton respectively. The Korean edition is precipitated by the desire to recover a national literature, seen as embodying national identity, and reflects a new canon that presently governs literary study in Korea and the West. The makers of this canon have tried to narrow the gap between written and spoken, refined and popular and to evaluate not only native works overlooked in the past but also works in literary Chinese once considered canonical but now neglected.

The present work, *The Columbia Anthology of Traditional Korean Poetry*, is based on the first volume of the Korean edition with certain deletions and additions. This volume on classical poetry offers a representative selection from the four major genres of native poetry: the Silla songs known as *hyangga* transcribed in *hyangch'al* orthographic system, some of which drew upon an oral tradition as old as the recorded history of the Korean people, Koryŏ songs, *sijo*, and *kasa*. Within each genre works are arranged chronologically so that the reader may trace the genre's development and note changes in topic, scale, voice, diction, point of view, and rhetorical pattern. Moreover, with the consent of the compilers, I have added a section of poetry written in literary Chinese—for poetry in Korea, regardless of the language used, was considered the pinnacle of literary art, especially poetry in Chinese, which every educated member of society studied and wrote. The anthology concludes with examples of orature—folk songs and shamanist narrative songs.

I would like to thank my collaborators for their contributions, especially Father Kevin O'Rourke for permission to include his translations of *sijo* and *sasŏl sijo* from his unpublished manuscript.

Finally, grateful acknowledgment is made for permission to include the following copyrighted material:

University of California Press, for selections from *The Bamboo Grove: An Introduction to Sijo*, copyright © 1971 the Regents of the University of California, with permission from Richard Rutt;

Columbia University Press, for selections from David McCann, *Early Korean Literature: Selections and Introductions*, copyright © 2000 Columbia University Press;

Harvard University Press, for selections from Peter H. Lee, *Songs of Flying Dragons: A Critical Reading*, copyright © 1975 the Harvard-Yenching Institute;

University of Hawaii Press, for selections from Peter H. Lee, ed., *Anthology of Korean Literature: From Early Times to the Nineteenth Century*, copyright © 1981 University Press of Hawaii, and *Pine River and Lone Peak: An Anthology of Three Chosŏn Dynasty Poets*, copyright © 1991 University of Hawaii Press;

Kevin O'Rourke, for selections from *Singing Like a Cricket, Hooting Like an Owl: Selected Poems of Yi Kyu-bo*, copyright © 1995 Kevin O'Rourke;

Kim Jong Gil, *Slow Chrysanthemums*, copyright © 1987 Chi-gyu Kim.

CONTRIBUTORS

CK   Chi-gyu Kim (Kim Chonggil), Korea University
CS   Carolyn So, formerly with Claremont McKenna College
DM   David R. McCann, Harvard University
OR   Kevin O'Rourke, Kyŏnghŭi University
PL   Peter H. Lee, University of California, Los Angeles
PP   Pori Park, Carleton College
RL   Richard J. Lynn, University of Toronto
RR   Richard Rutt, Falmouth, Cornwall, England
WH   Wen Hsia-min, University of Hawaii

CLASSICAL POETRY

INTRODUCTION

The performance of oral songs in the religious life of the ancient Korean people is vividly recorded in the Chinese dynastic histories. What struck the Chinese then—and will strike the reader now as well—is the Korean people's love of singing and dancing. At state assemblies the chief ritualist would tell the story of the divine origin of the founder, as evinced by foundation myths, and his extraordinary deeds in war and peace. Recited narrative was interspersed with primal song (*norae*) that not only welcomed, entertained, and sent off gods and spirits but also moved mountains and set all nature dancing in harmony. Thus orality and performance were significant features of vernacular poetry in traditional Korea. By oral I mean, with Paul Zumthor, any poetic communication "where transmission and reception at least are carried by voice and hearing"; by performance I mean "the complex action by which a poetic message is simultaneously transmitted and perceived in the here and now."[1]

The first recorded short song used as a means of incantation occurs in the third month of the year 42, when nine chiefs and several hundred people climbed Mount Kuji to greet the sovereign and joyfully sang the "Song of Welcoming the Divine Lord" (*Kuji ka* or *Yŏng singun ka*)—invoking King Suro's descent. This song, or spell, was not composed in writing but comes down to us transcribed into Chinese. Seven hundred years later, in the early eighth century, another song was sung by the common people when Lady Suro was abducted by a dragon. Lady Suro was the wife of Lord Sunjŏng, who was on his way to his post as governor of Kangnŭng. When the entourage did not know what to do, there appeared an old man who said, "An old saying has it that many mouths can melt even iron. Even

1. Paul Zumthor, *Oral Poetry: An Introduction* (Minneapolis: University of Minnesota Press, 1990), pp. 23 and 22.

the sea monster is bound to be afraid of many mouths. Gather the people from the area, compose and sing a song, and strike a hill with sticks. Then you will regain your wife." The song, issuing from the mouth with phonic and rhythmic richness, with immediacy and transparency of the text, proclaimed an urgent message through the human voice. This collective performance reaffirms the mythic value of live voice and the belief that song can move gods and spirits.

Like all subsequent classic vernacular poetic forms in Korea, the first genre covered here, the *hyangga*, were sung. The forms and styles of Korean poetry therefore reflect its melodic origins. The basis of its prosody is a line consisting of metric segments of three or four syllables, the rhythm most natural to the language. In the ten-line *hyangga* the ninth line usually begins with an interjection that indicates heightened emotions, a change in tempo and pitch, and presages the poem's conclusion. Musical notations indicate that the musical divisions of the next genre, the popular Koryŏ song, signaled by an interjection followed by a refrain, are different from its poetic (stanzaic) divisions. Furthermore, the association of verbal and musical rhythms can be seen in the refrain of Koryŏ songs. Nonsense jingles or onomatopoetic representations of the sounds of such musical instruments as the drum, gong, or double-reed oboe attest to the refrain's musical origins and function. The characteristic songs of Koryŏ were all performed and transmitted orally until the sixteenth century when music books recorded the texts and tunes. The survival of Koryŏ song texts is due to the adoption of accompanying music for use at court from the beginning of the fifteenth century. *Sijo*, the third and most popular vernacular poetic genre, were sung, commonly taking over two minutes for a three-line text. Some *sijo* were simultaneously composed and performed, but others were written to be sung by female entertainers or servants. *Kasa*, the fourth vernacular poetic genre, were recited or chanted.

Those associated with the oral performance of vernacular poetry in Korea included shamans, Buddhist monks, members of the elite corps of *hwarang* (along with the monks, the most educated members of Silla society at one time), female slaves and entertainers, musicians, servants of both sexes, and professional singers, who acted as composers/singers/interpreters from the eighteenth century. But records indicate that after Silla those entrusted with performance were members of the lower classes, such as female entertainers, shamans, servants, and artisans. It was deemed undignified for members of the ruling elite to perform. In Korea the performance, distribution, and transmission of vernacular poetry was almost exclusively enacted by women, who were often marginalized and oppressed by the ruling elite.

A word should be said about the translation of Silla and Koryŏ songs. The compiler of volume 1 of the Korean edition offers two readings of Silla songs by Yang Chudong (1903–1977) and Kim Wanjin (b. 1931), but variant readings are proposed by other philologists. A similar difficulty arises in the study of Koryŏ songs. Ambiguous or obsolete words present problems in dividing and interpreting words and phrases—as, for example, in "Song of Green Mountain." The interpretation of a word often depends on one's deciphering of another word or on the context. Some commentators follow a mere hunch and hit upon novel readings—what Hanning terms "textual harassment . . . the forcible imposition of special meanings on single words or entire verbal structures."[2] In view of such cruxes, I have offered a reading that is philologically accurate and poetically adequate. Alternative readings are given in notes.

2. Robert W. Hanning, "'I Shal Finde It in a Maner Close': Versions of Textual Harassment in Medieval Literature," in Laurie A. Finke and Martin B. Schichtman, eds., *Medieval Texts and Contemporary Readers* (Ithaca: Cornell University Press, 1987), p. 27.

HYANGGA

The term *"hyangga"* (native songs) designates Korean songs as opposed to poetry written in classical Chinese (*si*). This genre specifically covers the extant twenty-five songs dating from Silla and early Koryŏ, transcribed in the *hyangch'al* orthographic system, in which Chinese graphs are used phonetically and semantically to represent the sounds of Old Korean.[1]

Great Master Iryŏn (1206–1289), the compiler of the *Memorabilia of the Three Kingdoms* (*Samguk yusa*, 1285), provides prose settings for fourteen song texts adequate for appreciation of a given song. But in some cases he lumps this information under one heading—under the monk/*hwarang*/poet Ch'ungdam (fl. 742–765) for two very different songs, for example, and Ch'ŏyong, who accompanied King Hŏngang (875–886) to help in state affairs. The translation gives a summary of Iryŏn's introductory note.

Eighteen of the twenty-five *hyangga* presented here are Buddhist in inspiration and content, reflecting certain trends in Silla and Koryŏ Buddhism: belief in the Pure Land of Maitreya and Amitāyus (Infinite Life) in "Prayer to Amitāyus," "Song of Tuṣita Heaven," and "Requiem for the Dead Sister"; belief in the Sound Observer in "Hymn to the Thousand-Eyed Sound Observer." Great Master Kyunyŏ (923–973), a learned monk/poet who revived the Flower Garland school in the tenth

---

1. Of the three variants of *hyangga*, the most polished and popular form consisted of two stanzas of four lines plus a two-line conclusion (*hugu, nakku, kyŏkku*; eighteen songs). Konishi Jin'ichi points out the close relationship between the *hyangch'al* and the Japanese *Man'yōgana* and between the *hugu* and the envoy to long poems (*chōka*) in the early period of the *Collection of Ten Thousand Leaves* (*Man'yōshū*; c. 759). *A History of Japanese Literature*, vol. 1: *The Archaic and Ancient Ages*, trans. Aileen Gatten and Nicholas Teele (Princeton: Princeton University Press, 1984), pp. 334–335.

century, composed eleven songs, taught them orally, and encouraged the congregation to chant and memorize them. Of the remaining *hyangga*, one finds here a folk song, a work song, a Buddhist charm to Maitreya, songs in praise of Silla's elite corps of knights (*hwarang*), a shamanist song, a song about a breach of promise, and a song about statesmanship.

Although the composer and performer are one and the same person in only four cases, one can assume from the context that other songs were performed as well. From the social context of performance and the nature of the audience we can imagine the personality of the performer and the style of the performance itself. Several were recognized for their talent in composing: five named monks, some of whom served the *hwarang* as chaplains entrusted with religious education and teaching of such Confucian virtues as loyalty, filial piety, and sincerity, a nameless old man, the mother of a blind boy, a disappointed official, and Ch'ŏyong (believed to be a son of the Dragon King). Some songs were performed and transmitted until the time of Iryŏn in the thirteenth century—for example, "A Folk Song" ("P'ungyo"; c. 635), an anonymous song to praise the eminent monk Yangji, sung when performing repetitive tasks such as pounding rice and constructing buildings. Unlike other vernacular genres with extant musical notations, no musical settings for Silla songs are extant. Nor do multiple versions of the same song text survive, as they do, for example, in *sijo*.

KING MU OF PAEKCHE (600–641)

Song of Sŏdong

A widow who lived on the shores of the southern lake near the Paekche capital had a child by a water dragon. The child was named Chang. Since he used to live by selling the yams he dug, he was known as Sŏdong (Yam Boy). Hearing of the beauty of the third princess, Sŏnhwa, of King Chinp'yŏng (579–632) of Silla, he shaved his head and came to the Silla capital. Because he gave yams to the children, they liked him and followed him. He then wrote the following song and had the children sing it—a song so popular that it spread throughout the capital and reached even the royal palace. Because of it the princess was then exiled, and on her way to the place of exile, Sŏdong appeared and escorted her. When they made love, she learned that he was Sŏdong himself and became convinced of the song's efficacy. Together they went to Paekche and were married. And eventually Sŏdong became king and was known as King Mu of Paekche.

Princess Sŏnhwa,
After a secret affair,
Steals away at night,
With Sŏdong in her arms.

MASTER YUNGCH'ŎN (C. 579–632)

Song of the Comet

During the reign of King Chinp'yŏng, three members of the *hwarang*, Kŏyŏl, Silch'ŏ (or Tolch'ŏ), and Podong, were about to make an excursion to the Diamond Mountains when a comet violated Scorpius, a star in one of the twenty-eight lunar mansions. Filled with foreboding, the three were about to abandon their plans. Then Master Yungch'ŏn composed a song (dated 594), whereupon the uncanny comet disappeared and thus turned a misfortune into a blessing. The king was pleased and had the three youths go to the mountains.

> There is castle by the Eastern Sea
> Where once a mirage used to play.
> Japanese soldiers came,
> Torches were burnt in the forest.[2]

> When knights visited this mountain,
> The moon marked its westerly course,
> And a star was about to sweep a path,
> Someone said, "Look, there is a comet!"

> Ah, the moon has already departed.
> Now, where shall we look for the long-tailed star?

2. Or: on the frontier.

ANONYMOUS

Ode to Yangji (c. 635)

While an enlightened monk named Yangji was casting a sixteen-foot Buddha statue for Yŏngmyo Monastery, men and women carried clay singing this song.

We have come, have come, have come,
How sad, we have come!
Sad are the living beings,
We have come to garner merit.

KWANGDŎK (FL. 661–681)

Prayer to Amitāyus

Kwangdŏk, a celibate ascetic, lived in the village of West Punhwang and endeavored to practice virtue. He is said to have gone to the Western Paradise of Amitāyus, as he had prayed.

O moon,
Go to the West, and
Pray to Amitāyus
And tell

That there is one who
Adores the Buddha of Infinite Life and
Longs for the Pure Land,
Praying before Him with folded hands.

Ah, would he leave me out
When he fulfills the forty-eight vows?[3]

3. Vows on rebirth in the Pure Land of Amitābha.

TŬGO (FL. 692–702)

Ode to Knight Chukchi

All living beings sorrow and lament
Over the spring that is past;
Your face once fair and bright
Is about to wear deep furrows.

I must glimpse you
Even for an awesome moment.
My fervent mind cannot rest at night
In the mugwort-rank hollow.

AN OLD MAN (C. 702–732)

Dedication

On the way to his new post, Lord Sunjŏng happened to eat lunch by the beach. Looking at an azalea blooming on the cliff, his wife, Lady Suro, asked for the flower, but nobody dared climb to the top of the cliff. At that time an old man leading a cow happened to pass by and, hearing the lady's wishes, picked the azaleas for her with this song.

If you would let me leave
The cow tethered to the brown rock,
And feel no shame for me,
I would pluck and dedicate the flowers!

SINCH'UNG (FL. 737–742)

Regret

Sinch'ung used to play chess with the future king Hyosŏng (737–742) under a pine tree. The prince vowed by the tree that he would not forget his friend. But, after ascending the throne, the king forgot about Sinch'ung, who then composed this song (737) and fixed it to the tree. Then, suddenly, the tree died. The king regretted his lapse of memory and conferred a title on his erstwhile friend.

You said you would no more forget me
Than the densely green pine
Would wither in the fall.
That familiar face is there still.

The moon in the ancient lake
Complains of the transient tide.
I still glimpse your figure,
But how I dislike this world.[4]

4. Or: Now I reproach the world.

MASTER WŎLMYŎNG (C. 742–765)

Song of Tuṣita Heaven

At the request of King Kyŏngdŏk, Master Wŏlmyŏng composed this song in 760 to remove two suns that had appeared in the sky. The transcription reads: "On the Dragon Tower I sing a song of scattering flowers and send a petal to the blue cloud. In place of my sincere wish, go and welcome the Great Sage in the Tuṣita Heaven."

O flowers, strewn today
With a song. Since you attend
My honest mind's command,
You serve Maitreya!

Requiem for the Dead Sister

In memory of his sister, Master Wŏlmyŏng offered a ceremony of abstinence with this song. A gust of wind then blew the paper money offerings to the west.

On the hard road of life and death
That is near our land,
You went, afraid,
Without words.

We know not where we go,
Leaves blown, scattered,
Though fallen from the same tree,
By the first winds of autumn.

Ah, I will polish the path
Until I meet you in the Pure Land.

MASTER CH'UNGDAM (C. 742–765)

Statesmanship

On the third day of the third month of 765, King Kyŏngdŏk asked that a virtuous monk be brought to him. At that time the master in patched clothes appeared from the south. At the king's request for a song about the art of government, the master composed this lyric.

The king is father,
And his ministers are loving mothers.
His subjects are foolish children;
They only receive what love brings.

Schooled in saving the masses,
The king feeds and guides them.
Then no one will desert this land—
This is the way to govern a country.

Peace and prosperity will prevail if each—
King, minister, and subject—lives as he should.

Ode to Knight Kip'a

This song was known for its intense emotion and noble spirit, and King Kyŏngdŏk himself praised it highly. It has no introductory note by Iryŏn.

The moon that pushes her way
Through the thickets of clouds,
Is she not pursuing
The white clouds?

Knight Kip'a once stood by the water,
Reflecting his face in the Iro.
Henceforth I shall seek and gather
The depth of his mind among pebbles.

Knight, you are the towering pine
That scorns frost, ignores snow.

HŬIMYŎNG (FL. 742–765)

Hymn to the Thousand-Eyed Sound Observer

Hŭimyŏng composed this song on behalf of her five-year-old blind son and had him recite it and pray.

Falling on my knees,
Pressing my hands together,
Thousand-Eyed Sound Observer,[5]
I implore thee.

Yield me,
Who lacks,
One among your thousand eyes;
By your mystery restore me whole.

If you grant me one of your many eyes,
Oh, the bounty, then, of your charity.

5. *Kwanŭm,* the bodhisattva who observes the sounds of the world.

MONK YŎNGJAE (C. 785–798)

Meeting Bandits

Intending to spend his last days on South Peak in retirement, the monk Yŏngjae was crossing the Taehyŏn Ridge when he met sixty thieves. The bandits drew their swords and threatened him. But since they had heard of his reputation as a poet, they asked him to compose an impromptu song.

The day I did not know
My true mind—
Now I am awakened from ignorance
And am going through the forest.[6]

Transgressors hiding in the bushes,
You can turn your merits to save others.
If I'm stabbed to death,
Then a good day will dawn.[7]

Ah, such a meager good deed
Cannot build a lofty edifice.

6. Lines 3–4 can also be read: And am on my way hidden / To cultivate the Path.

7. Lines 5–8 can also be read: How can I revert to the state / Where I fear the fallen transgressors? / If I endure these spears and swords, / A good day will dawn.

CH'ŏYONG (FL. 875–886)

Song of Ch'ŏyong

Ch'ŏyong, one of the seven sons of the Dragon King of the Eastern Sea, married a beautiful woman. Seeing that she was extremely desirable, an evil spirit transformed himself into a man and attacked her in her room while Ch'ŏyong was away. But when Ch'ŏnyong returned and witnessed the scene, he calmly sang the following song, which so moved the evil spirit that it went away. Later, the Ch'ŏyong mask was used to exorcise evil spirits, usually on New Year's Eve.

Having caroused far into the night
In the moonlit capital,
I return home and in my bed,
Behold, four legs.

Two were mine,
Whose are the other two?
Formerly two were mine;
What shall be done now they are taken?

GREAT MASTER KYUNYŎ (923–973)

Eleven Poems on the Ten Vows of the Universally Worthy Bodhisattva

Great Master Kyunyŏ was a learned monk who single-handedly revived the Flower Garland school in the tenth century. A prolific commentator and popularizer of Buddhism, he composed songs in the vernacular, taught them orally, and encouraged the congregation to chant and memorize them. The text is preserved in chapter 7 of the *Life of Kyunyŏ* (1075). A Chinese translation was made by Ch'oe Heanggwi in 967.

The contents of the songs are as follows: 1. worshiping and honoring the Buddha, 2. praise of the Thus Come One, 3. wide cultivation and the making of offerings, 4. repentance for sins, 5. rejoicing in the merit of others, 6. entreaty for turning the dharma wheel, 7. entreaty for the Buddha to live in this world, 8. constant following of the Buddha's teaching, 9. constant harmony with the living, 10. transfer of merit, and 11. conclusion.

1   I bow before the buddhas
Whom I draw with my mind's brush.
O this body of mine,
Reach the end of the dharma realm.

Every mote of dust is a Buddha land.
Every Buddha realm worships the buddhas
Who fill the dharma realm—
I will worship them throughout the nine time periods.

Ah, untiring in the deeds of body, speech, thought—
I have made this my credo.

2 "Homage to the buddhas."
   So speak the tongues today.
   O sea of inexhaustible eloquence—
   Gush forth from a single thought.

   We hail you, achiever of merit;
   We praise you, Medicine King,
   With your boundless ocean of virtue,
   Who exist in dust and empty space.

   Ah, would that my tongue could praise
   An infinitesimal part of your virtue.

3 With tongs I trim the lamp
   That burns before the Buddha and pray:
   "The wick become large as Mount Sumeru
   And the oil become a great ocean."

   The incense reaches beyond the dharma realm,
   Every incense an offering
   To the buddhas who fill the dharma realm—
   I offer them many offerings.

   Ah, the offerings of the dharma are many:
   But this indeed is the greatest.

4 I have committed errors
   And strayed from the path to bodhi.
   All my evil deeds
   Bar me from the realm of dharma.

   I've fallen into evil deeds, words, and thoughts,
   But will cherish the lord of pure precepts.
   Know the buddhas of ten directions
   That today I have truly repented.

   Ah, when the realm of living ends, my penance ends.
   May I forever abandon evil karma.

5   The truth of dependent origination tells me
That illusion and enlightenment are one.
From the buddhas to living beings,
There cannot be one who is not myself.

What the Buddha practices is what I practice,
What the Buddha attains is what I attain.
So how could I not rejoice
In the good deeds of others?

Ah, when I practice so,
How could the jealous mind be aroused?

6   To the majestic assembly of buddhas
In the dharma realm,
I go forth and pray
For the dharma rain.

Disperse the blight of affliction
Rooted deep in the soil of ignorance,
And wet the mind's fields of living beings,
Where good grasses struggle to grow.

Ah, how happy is a moonlit autumn field,
Ripe with the fruit of knowledge.

7   Though all the buddhas
Have fulfilled the purpose of their coming,
I will join my palms and pray
That they will remain in the world.

From bright dawn to dark night,
I have found a friend who will intercede for us.
Knowing this truth,
How sad those who have gone astray.

Ah, were the water of our minds clean,
His reflected image should shine there.

8   I will at once follow the vows
     That our buddhas cultivated in the past
     And practiced with great hardship,
     With arduous progress and vigor.

     When this body crumbles and turns to dust,
     When I offer my life completely,
     I would joyfully follow the vows
     That all the buddhas have fulfilled.

     O mind that cultivates the Buddha's path,
     May it not stray to another path.

9   The king of the bodhi tree
     Takes the deluded as roots.
     With his water of great mercy
     He moistens them lest they wither.

     I shall serve the living teeming in the dharma realm
     As I do the buddhas,
     Whether I live or die
     In every thought without pause.

     Ah, the day the living are at peace,
     The buddhas too will rejoice.

10   Would that all my good deeds
     Might be transferred to others.
     I would like to awaken those
     Wandering in the ocean of living beings.

     When we attain the ocean of buddhahood,
     Repented evil deeds are jewels
     In the dharma nature.
     It has been thus since aeons ago.

     Ah, the buddhas I worship are
     To be found in me and others.

11 When the realm of living runs out,
My vows, too, will have been acted out.
To enlighten the living beings
Is the boundless ocean of his vows.

Since I strive and progress so,
Each way I tread is a path to good deeds.
These are the vows of the Universally Worthy,
They are also the work of buddhas.

Ah, let's fathom the Universally Worthy's mind
And follow his single path.

P L

KORYŎ SONGS

Koryŏ songs (*sogyo*) are characterized by a recurrent refrain that reflects their folk and musical origins and their oral transmission. They were performed and transmitted orally until the sixteenth century when music books such as *Notations for Korean Music in Contemporary Use* (*Siyong hyangak po*)—the first systematic musical notation, providing both written music and written words—recorded them in the Korean alphabet. The survival of Koryŏ song texts results from their adoption as musical accompaniment for use at court from the beginning of the Chosŏn dynasty (1392–1910). Because no other music was available at the time, the popular eulogies compiled to celebrate the founding of the new dynasty were sung to the tune of popular Koryŏ songs. Whether Koryŏ songs were all composed orally is uncertain, but there was an interaction between oral and written forms and high and low.

These songs, like other vernacular poetic genres in Korea, depend on several expressive strategies: parataxis (juxtaposition of elements without subordinating them), the recurrence of such textual elements as formulas, parallelism, repetition, refrains, and nonsense jingles, and various kinds of sound symbolism. Most meaningless refrains are thought to be onomatopoeic imitations of instrumental sounds, such as the drum, gong, or double-reed oboe, or to mark instrumental interludes. The refrain is an indispensable element in chain verse, by means of which a song consisting of several independent parts with different contents is unified. For in most Koryŏ songs each stanza can be read as an independent unit. It is the refrain that links the individual units, so that each stanza can play its role in achieving the final effect. It should be noted, however, that some Koryŏ songs do not have stanzaic divisions: in these songs several different units are linked together— as, for example, in the "Song of Ch'ŏyong," which consists of six parts, including the song written in 879.

Clear marking of the lyric persona and the abundance of honorific verbal endings indicate the gender not only of the lyric speaker but that of the performer—female slaves, entertainers, shamans—as well as the place of performance: the court, often in the presence of the king. And the occasion of performance sometimes transformed the longing for the beloved in the original into that for the lord or king. Another device was to add elements of praise to camouflage the realistic contents to suit the occasion—as in "Ode to the Seasons."

Most of these songs sing of love. Favorite topics concern the pathos of separation and desertion more than the celebration of love. Love is mutable, illusory, and nothing can assuage the heart's sufferings. Indeed love was the privileged topic of women in vernacular songs.

The "Song of the Gong and Chimes" sings of an unbroken dynastic line and prays that the king's life lasts as long as heaven and earth. After offering a series of impossibilities, the song then declares that only if these ever occur shall "we part from the virtuous lord." The use of the topic of impossibilities (*adynaton*) as a rhetorical device in the poetry of praise is commonplace in Korea as elsewhere. In addition, this section of the book presents folk songs such as "Maternal Love," "Song of the Pigeon," "Song of the Pestle," and "Song of Chŏngŭp," which is said to date from Paekche but was still popular during the Koryŏ dynasty.

KING YEJONG (1079–1122)

Dirge for Two Generals

At the harvest festival (*P'algwanhoe*) held in the western capital, P'yŏngyang, in the tenth month of 1120, King Yejong saw two horses carrying two effigies prancing around the courtyard. Upon inquiry, the king learned they were the images of two generals, Sin Sunggyŏm and Kim Nak, who had sacrificed their lives to save Wang Kŏn (918–943), the founder of the Koryŏ dynasty. Deeply moved, the king composed this poem.

Loyal hearts that saved your king
Reach the end of heaven.
Though your souls departed,
You stand erect and speak.[1]

O two heroes of merit!
I know
The trace of your loyalty
Endures throughout the ages.

1. Or: You've received great honor.

CHŎNG SŎ (C. 1151–1170)

Regret

At the place of his exile, Tongnae, Chŏng is said to have composed this poem ("Chŏng Kwajŏng") plucking the black zither.

I who have yearned for you and wept
Am like a bird in the hills.[2]
Ah, that their false words were wrong,
May my soul be there where yours resides, ah!
Who opposed you?[3]
I've committed no errors or crime.
They are all lies.
How sad, ah![4]
Have you already forgotten me?
Listen to me, O lord, show me favor.

2. Or cuckoo.
3. Or: Who insisted on my crime?
4. Or: I wish I were dead.

ANONYMOUS

Ode to the Seasons

Virtue in a rear cup,
Happiness in a front cup,
Come to offer
Virtue and happiness![5]
Aŭ tongdong tari

The river in January *aŭ*[6]
Now freezes, now melts.
Born into this world,
I live alone.
Aŭ tongdong tari

You are like a lofty lantern *aŭ*
High up in the air.
In mid-February,
Your figure shines upon the world.
Aŭ tongdong tari

5. Stanza 1 also reads: With virtue in one hand, / And happiness in the other, / Come, come, you gods / With virtue and happiness. / *Aŭ tongdong tari*

Or: We offer virtue to gods / And happiness to ancestors. / We have come to offer / Virtue and happiness.

Or: Let's offer virtue to gods, / Let's offer happiness to ancestors. / Virtue and fortune / We've come to offer.

6. In the original the first lunar month that corresponds to the Western February-March. I have used the Western month throughout, because it is more direct and less awkward than, for example, "mid-second month." In East Asia the four seasons were regarded as consisting of three months each.

In March *aŭ*
Plums[7] bloom in late spring.
Others envy
Your magnificent figure!
Aŭ tongdong tari

In April without forgetting *aŭ*
Orioles, you've come.
But you, my clerk,
Forget bygone days.
Aŭ tongdong tari

On the feast of irises *aŭ*
I brew healing herbs
And offer you this drink—
May you live a thousand years.
Aŭ tongdong tari

On a mid-June day *aŭ*
I'm like a comb cast from a cliff!
Even for a moment I'll follow you
Who will look after me.
Aŭ tongdong tari

In mid-July *aŭ*
On the feast of the dead,
I prepare dainties of land and sea
And pray that we may be together.[8]
Aŭ tongdong tari

This is the full moon, *aŭ*
Of the mid-autumn festival.
This will be the festive day
If only I am with you.
Aŭ tongdong tari

7. Or azaleas.
8. Also reads: In mid-July *aŭ* / I plant many kinds of seeds / And pray / That I
may go with you.

On the double ninth *aŭ*
We eat yellow flowers.
O fragrance of chrysanthemums,
The season's change is late.[9]
Aŭ tongdong tari

In October *aŭ*
I'm like a sliced berry.
Once the branch is broken,
Who will cherish it?
Aŭ tongdong tari

On a November night *aŭ*
I lie on a dirt floor
With only a sheet to cover me.
O lonely life, night without you.
Aŭ tongdong tari

In December I am like *aŭ*
Chopsticks carved from pepperwood
Placed neatly before you:
An unknown guest holds them.
Aŭ tongdong tari

9. Or: The thatched village is quiet.

Song of Ch'ŏyong

After the event of the year 879, when Ch'ŏyong drove away the evil spirit, his mask was used by the people to expel demons and pestilence. This choral dance was performed at court on New Year's Eve to exorcise evil spirits from the country.

In the glorious reign of Silla, calm and bright,
We owe this peaceful era to the grace of Rāhu.
Father Ch'ŏyong,[10]
If he never talks to us,
If he never talks to us,
Three calamities and eight difficulties
Will vanish all at once.
O his bearing,
Ch'ŏyong's bearing,
Head, inclining under adorned flowers,
Oh, the brow that manifests longevity,
Thick eyebrows, imbued with the mountain spirit,
Eyes perfect from having gazed lovingly at humans,
Dented ears, gardens full of music,
Face pink as peach blossoms.
Deeply set nose[11] that smelled the five incenses,
O indulgent mouth, having received a thousand gold pieces,
Teeth like white jade or glass,

10. Refers affectionately to a son of the Dragon King, the author of "Song of Ch'ŏyong" (879).
11. Or: Prominent nose.

Chin, slightly curved, praised for good fortune,
Shoulders, stooped under the seven jewels,
Sleeves, hanging down, flooded with overpowering blessings,[12]
Breast, endowed with wisdom and virtue,
Stomach, full with happiness and wisdom,
Waist, bent with the striking pink sash,
O long legs, because he enjoys peace with others,
And his feet, wide from visiting his clients![13]
Who has made, who has made,
Without a needle, without thread,
Without a needle, without thread,
Who has fashioned Father Ch'ŏyong?
Many, many have created him,
How great, how imposing!
Twelve kingdoms put him together.
Oh, many have made Father Ch'ŏyong.

Cherries, crab apples, green plums
Come out to tie my sandals,[14]
If you do not, I'll curse you.[15]

Having caroused far into the night
In the moonlit capital,
I return home and in my bed
Behold four legs.
Oh, two were mine;
Whose are the other two?

Think now, if Ch'ŏyong sees you,
O demon of pestilence, he'll cut you to pieces.

Shall we offer you thousands of gold pieces,
Father Ch'ŏyong?

12. Or: Heavy with a string atop the sleeve.
13. Or: Holding shamanist rituals.
14. Or: To heal my scabs.
15. Or: Awful words will descend.

Shall we offer you the seven jewels,
Father Ch'ŏyong?

Not the gold, nor the jewels,
Catch me that demon, catch him.

Over the mountains, over the fields,
Avoid Ch'ŏyong far away.

Oh, that was the plea of the demon.

O CHAM (FL. 1274–1308)

The Turkish Bakery

I go to the Turkish shop, buy a bun,
An old Turk grasps me by the hand.
If this story is spread abroad,
tarorŏ kŏdirŏ You alone are to blame, little actor!
Tŏrŏ tungsyŏng tarirŏdirŏ tarirŏdirŏ tarorŏgŏdirŏ tarorŏ
I too will go to his bed:
Wi wi tarorŏ kŏdirŏ tarorŏ[16]
A narrow place, sultry and dark.

I go to Samjang Temple to light the lantern,
A chief priest grasps me by the hand.
If this story is spread abroad,
You alone are to blame, little altar boy!
I too will go to his bed:
A narrow place, sultry and dark.

I go to the well to draw water,
A dragon within grasps me by the hand.
If this story is spread abroad,
You alone are to blame, dipper!
I too will go to his bed:
A narrow place, sultry and dark.

I go to the tavern to buy the wine,
An innkeeper grasps me by the hand.

16. Refrains omitted from stanza 2.

If this story is spread abroad,
You alone are to blame, wine jug!
I too will go to his bed:
A narrow place, sultry and dark.

Song of P'yŏngyang

P'yŏngyang *ajŭlkka*
Although P'yŏngyang is my capital
Wi tuŏrŏngsyŏng tuŏrŏngsyŏng taringdiri

I love *ajŭlkka*
Although I love the repaired city,
Wi tuŏrŏngsyŏng tuŏrŏngsyŏng taringdiri

Instead of parting *ajŭlkka*
Instead of parting I'd rather stop spinning
Wi tuŏrŏngsyŏng tuŏrŏngsyŏng taringdiri

If you love me *ajŭlkka*
If you love me I'll follow you with tears
Wi tuŏrŏngsyŏng tuŏrŏngsyŏng taringdiri

Pearls *ajŭlkka*
Were the pearls to fall on the rock
Wi tuŏrŏngsyŏng tuŏrŏngsyŏng taringdiri

Would the thread *ajŭlkka*
Would the thread be broken?
Wi tuŏrŏngsyŏng tuŏrŏngsyŏng taringdiri

A thousand years *ajŭlkka*
If I parted from you a thousand years
Wi tuŏrŏngsyŏng tuŏrŏngsyŏng taringdiri

Would my heart *ajŭlkka*
Would my heart be changed?
Wi tuŏrŏngsyŏng tuŏrŏngsyŏng taringdiri

Taedong River *ajŭlkka*
Not knowing how wide the river is
Wi tuŏrŏngsyŏng tuŏrŏngsyŏng taringdiri

You pushed the boat off *ajŭlkka*
You pushed the boat off, boatman!
Wi tuŏrŏngsyŏng tuŏrŏngsyŏng taringdiri

Your own wife *ajŭlkka*
Not knowing how loose your wife is
Wi tuŏrŏngsyŏng tuŏrŏngsyŏng taringdiri

You board the ferry *ajŭlkka*
You had my love board the ferry, boatman!
Wi tuŏrŏngsyŏng tuŏrŏngsyŏng taringdiri

Taedong River *ajŭlkka*
The flower beyond the Taedong River
Wi tuŏrŏngsyŏng tuŏrŏngsyŏng taringdiri

When he has crossed the shore *ajŭlkka*
When he has crossed he will pluck another flower!
Wi tuŏrŏngsyŏng tuŏrŏngsyŏng taringdiri

Song of P'yŏngyang Without Refrain

Although P'yŏngyang is my capital,
Although I love the repaired city,
Instead of parting I'd rather stop spinning
If you love me I'll follow you with tears.

Were the pearls to fall on the rock,
Would the thread be broken?
If I parted from you a thousand years,
Would my heart be changed?

Not knowing how wide the river is,
You pushed the boat off, boatman.
Not knowing how loose your wife is,
You had my love board the ferry, boatman.

The flower beyond the Taedong River,
When he has crossed the shore
When he has crossed he will pluck another flower!

Song of Green Mountain

Let's live, let's live,
Let's live on the green mountain!
With wild grapes and thyme,
Let's live on the green mountain!
Yalli yalli yallasyŏng yallari yalla

Cry, cry, birds,
Cry after you wake.
I've more sorrow than you
And cry after I wake.
Yalli yalli yallasyŏng yallari yalla

I see the bird passing, bird passing,
I see the passing bird beyond the waters.
With a mossy plow
I see the passing bird beyond the waters.
Yalli yalli yallasyŏng yallari yalla

I've spent the day
This way and that.
But where no man comes or goes,
How am I to pass the night?
Yalli yalli yallasyŏng yallari yalla

Where is this stone thrown?
At whom is this stone thrown?
Here no one to hate or love,
I am hit and I cry.
Yalli yalli yallasyŏng yallari yalla

Let's live, let's live,
Let's live by the sea!
With seaweed, oysters, and clams,
Let's live by the sea!
Yalli yalli yallasyŏng yallari yalla

I've listened as I went, went,
Turning an isolated kitchen I've listened.
I've listened to the stag fiddling
Perched on a bamboo pole.
Yalli yalli yallasyŏng yallari yalla

I have brewed strong wine
In a round-bellied jar.
A gourdlike leaven seizes me.
What shall I do now?
Yalli yalli yallasyŏng yallari yalla

Song of the Gong and Chimes

Ring the gong, strike the chimes!
Ring the gong, strike the chimes!
Let's enjoy this age of peace.[17]

On a brittle sandy cliff,
On a brittle sandy cliff,
Let's plant roasted chestnuts, five pints.

When the chestnuts shoot and sprout,
When the chestnuts shoot and sprout,
Then we'll part from the virtuous lord.

Let's carve a lotus out of jade,
Let's carve a lotus out of jade,
And graft the lotus in the stone.

When it blossoms in the winter,
When it blossoms in the winter,
Then we'll part from the virtuous lord.

Let's make an iron suit of armor,
Let's make an iron suit of armor,
Stitch the pleats with iron thread.

17. Or: Let's perform our duty in this age of peace.

When it has been worn and torn,
When it has been worn and torn,
Then we'll part from the virtuous lord.

Let's make an iron ox and put him,
Let's make an iron ox and put him,
To graze among the iron trees.

When he grazes the iron grass,
When he grazes the iron grass,
Then we'll part from the virtuous lord.

Were the pearls to fall on the rock,
Were the pearls to fall on the rock,
Would the thread be broken?

If I parted from you for a thousand years,
If I parted from you for a thousand years,
Would my heart be changed?

Treading Frost

After a rain, ah, comes a thick snow.
Do you come, who made me
Tarong tiusyŏ madŭksari madunŏjŭse nŏuji
Lie awake half the night,
Through a pass in the tangled wood,
Through an awful path to sleep?[18]

At times thunderbolts, ah,
My body will fall in to the Avīci hell[19]
And perish at once—
At times thunderbolts, ah,
My body will fall into the Avīci hell
And perish at once—
Would I walk on a different mountain path?[20]

Let's do this or that,
Is your pledge this or that?
Ah, love, living with you is my vow.

18. Lines 2 and 4–6 also read: On a path in the tangled wood [or thick with frost], / I think of my love / Who kept me awake all night. / Who'd come by this awful path to sleep?
19. Avīci, the last of the eight hot hells.
20. Or: Would I seek another lover's bosom?

Maternal Love

Hoe too is an edged tool,
But in sharpness sickle certainly wins.
Father too is a parent,
Wi tŏngdŏ tungsyŏng
But in love mother surely surpasses.
O love, his indeed cannot be more than hers.

Will You Go?

Will you go away?
Will you forsake me and go?
wi chŭngjulka O age of great peace and plenty![21]

How can you tell me to live on
And forsake me and go away?
O age of great peace and plenty!

I could stop you but fear
You would be annoyed and never return.
O age of great peace and plenty!

I'll let you go, wretched love,
But return as soon as you leave.
O age of great peace and plenty!

21. From stanza 2 I have omitted the refrain *wi chŭngjulka* whose meaning is unclear.

Spring Overflows the Pavilion

Were I to build a bamboo hut on the ice
And die of cold with him on the ice,
Were I to build a bamboo hut on the ice
And die of cold with him on the ice,
O night of our love, run slow, run slow.

When I lie alone, restless,
How can I fall asleep?
Only peach blossoms wave over the west window.
Ungrieved, you scorn the spring breeze,
Scorn the spring breeze.

I have cherished those who vowed,
"May my soul be with yours."
I have cherished those who vowed,
"May my soul be with yours."
Who, who persuaded me this was true?

"O duck, O duck,
O gentle duck,
Why do you come
To the swamp, instead of the shoal?"
"If the swamp freezes, the shoal will do, the shoal will do."

A bed on Mount South,
With Mount Jade as pillow
Mount Brocade as quilt,

And beside me a girl sweeter than musk,[22]
Let's press our magic hearts, press our magic hearts!

O love, let us be forever together!

22. Or: a girl with a pouch of musk.

Song of the Pestle

Let's mill grain with a rattle *hiyae*
Let's cook coarse rice *hiyae*
And offer it to father and mother *hiyahae*
If any remains I'll eat it *hiyahae*.

Song of the Pigeon

The pigeon
The pigeon
Can coo,
But I like
The cuckoo better
I like
The cuckoo better.

Song of Chŏngŭp

The wife of an itinerant merchant expresses her concern for her
husband's safety.

O moon, rise high,
And shine far and wide.
Ŏgiya ŏgangdyori
Aŭ tarongdiri
Are you at the marketplace?
Ah, may you not step onto wet ground.
Ŏgiya ŏgangdyori
Leave everything, whatever it is.
Ah, may darkness not overtake him.
Ŏgiya ŏgangdyori
Aŭ tarongdiri

PL

SONGS OF FLYING DRAGONS

Songs of Flying Dragons (*Yongbi ŏch'ŏn ka*, 1445–1447) is a monumental work among early Chosŏn eulogies: a cycle of 125 cantos comprising 248 poems. It was compiled on King Sejong's order to praise the founding of the Chosŏn dynasty by General Yi Sŏnggye (1335–1408), the king's grandfather, and to test the use of the new alphabet he had invented. Written by the foremost philologists and literary men in the Academy of Worthies, the *Songs* combine poetry and historiography to present the orthodox view of recent history. For the most part, the poems express themes of praise found in the classics and histories, highlighted with stylistic devices of comparison, amplification, parallelism, and formulas. Preparation began in 1437 with the gathering of accounts of deeds preserved in the veritable records as well as popular traditions circulating among the people. From October 1446 to March 1447 seven members of the academy completed the Korean verse; by February-March 1447 a ten-chapter commentary on the *Songs* was completed. Finally, on November 23, 1447, the king distributed 550 copies of the *Songs* to his subjects.

The first canto—which, together with the second, forms the prologue—sets the theme, mood, and purpose of the book: praise of the four ancestors and the first and third kings of the dynasty. These six dragons flying above the land of the Eastern Sea are Mokcho (d. 1274), Ikcho, Tojo (1367–1422), Hwanjo (1315–1361), Yi Sŏnggye (1335–1408), and Yi Pangwŏn (1367–1422). The central part of the book, cantos 3 to 124, is subdivided into two sections: the first, cantos 3–109, praises the cultural and military accomplishments of the six dragons; the second, cantos 110–124, consists of admonitions to future monarchs. Canto 125 is the conclusion. Each canto, except for cantos 1 and 125, consists of two poems, the first relating generally the great deeds of Chinese sovereigns and the second those of the Chosŏn kings (or their four ancestors). Cantos 86–89 are exceptions to the general scheme, since each poem celebrates the deeds of the founder. Cantos 108 and 109, the only cantos assigned to women, praise the exemplary deeds of the wife of King Wen, Queen Sinhye (wife of the founder of Koryŏ), and Queen Wŏngyŏng (wife of Yi Pangwŏn; 1365–1420). The compilers assigned five cantos to Mokcho, nine to Ikcho, four to Tojo, six to Hwanjo, eighty-one to Yi Sŏnggye, and twenty-three to Yi Pangwŏn.

A number of cantos (cantos 32, 43, 86, 88, and 89) celebrate Yi Sŏnggye's marksmanship. Yi wielded a huge bow, signifying his great military power, and his arrows made a whirring noise as they flew through the air. Like so many other heroes, Yi's companion in times of peace and war was a horse. He had eight stalwart steeds, all of which performed miracles of one sort or another. During peacetime, hunting trips, contests, or games provided him with occasions to perfect his horsemanship (cantos 44 and 63). With his supreme physical and spiritual qualities, Yi responded to calls to bring order and peace to a nation harassed by successive waves of foreign invaders: the Red Turbans in 1351, the Mongols in 1362 and 1370, and the Japanese pirates in 1377, 1380, and 1382 (cantos 47–52 and 58–62).

Yi Sŏnggye fulfilled the role of a Confucian soldier perfectly by withstanding the trials thrust upon him, responding bravely to the demand of a fate willed by heaven, and identifying his personal destiny with that of the nation. The ultimate justification of his military prowess, however, is his maintenance and preservation of order, as manifested in good government. The cantos that celebrate the statesmanship of Yi Sŏnggye, therefore, explore the nature and function of kingship, the relations of power and justice, the role of mercy and remonstrance, and the importance of learning and orthodoxy, culminating in the admonitory cantos that conclude the cycle (cantos 110–125).

The sovereign qualities of the Confucian king enumerated in the *Songs* recall the cardinal virtues of the Christian prince found in the "Mirror for Princes" literature. Yi Sŏnggye possessed the virtues of benevolence, justice tempered with mercy, learning, wisdom, temperance, compassion, modesty, and brotherly love. As the defender of moral order in the universe and a representative of his culture, the ruler's conduct brings about public order or public disorder. The compilers are therefore eager to illustrate public doctrine: the special qualifications required of a ruler and the particular functions he is expected to discharge for the good of the human community.

In the final section of the *Songs* the compilers directly address King Sejong. Through the earlier part the principal concern is the celebration of paradigmatic acts of the dynastic founder and the virtues he exemplifies—with the juxtaposition (and often integration) of native and classical materials becoming the source of resonance. In the final section, however, which consists of a series of gracious exhortations to the reigning monarch, we notice a shift to poignantly personal utterance that changes the focus from the distant and normative to the immediate and real. This effective variation of the compilers' strategy evinces the centrality, by the nature and tradition of their art, of the impulse to persuade.

The themes in this final section include the prevention and treatment of evils that arise from ease and luxury, the role of peace in breeding courage and resolve, the value of modesty and the harm of pride, the evils of flattery and slander, and the transforming power of virtue as the guardian of order. The final canto ends not only with a prophecy of national greatness but also with an allusive rhetorical question. Once again the compilers assert that the security of the throne depends entirely upon the ruler's worship of heaven and his dedication to the people. They then evoke the figure of T'ai K'ang of Hsia who, on his way back from a hunting trip, is said to have been ambushed by I, who subsequently seized the throne. T'ai K'ang's loss of the crown, caused by his indulgence in pleasures, shows how his personal conduct was the immediate source of public disorder. The primary element in constructing the total symbolic structure, however, lies in the meaning of the word *hunt*, a political metaphor for tyranny. The traditional associations of the hunt with war and games are familiar enough, but here emphasis is on the rapacity of the hunt and on the sportive tyrant whose prey included men. The hunt functions here as a metaphor for the unbounded energy of the tyrant, in disregard of the ideal political and moral order. Its admonitory appearance in the final canto warns against royal participation in such self-indulgent sport and outlines the cause-and-effect relationship between the moral energy of the ruler and the welfare of his state. Such was the figure of the ideal Confucian prince, whose lasting virtues were vital to the future of the dynasty.

Songs of Flying Dragons

1   Korea's six dragons flew in the sky.
    Their every deed was blessed by heaven.
    Their deeds tallied with those of sage kings.[1]

2   The tree, whose roots are deep,
    Is firm amidst the winds.
    Its flowers are good,
    Its fruits abundant.

    The stream, whose source is deep,
    Gushes forth even in a drought.
    It forms a river
    And gains the sea.

27   His arrow was huge beyond compare—
    His father saw it and abandoned it.
    On the same day he rejoiced
    In him whose genius astounded the day.[2]

32   Heaven sent a genius
    In order to save the people.
    Hence he shot with twenty arrows
    Twenty sables in the bush.

1. The six dragons are four ancestors Mokcho (d. 1274), Ikcho, Tojo (d. 1342), Hwanjo (1315–1360), Yi Sŏnggye (1392–1398), and Yi Pangwŏn (1400–1418).

2. From this canto only the second verse that deals with Korean kings is given. "His" refers to Yi Sŏnggye; "his father" refers to Hwanjo.

43 On Mount Chorae he struck two roebucks
   With a single arrow.
   Must one paint
   This natural genius?[3]

44 It was a polo match played by royal order—
   He hit the ball with a "sideways block." [4]
   People on nine state roads
   All admired his skill.

70 Heaven gave him courage and wisdom
   Who was to bring order to his country.
   Hence eight seeds
   Appeared at the proper time.[5]

86 He shot six roebucks,
   He shot six crows,
   He flew across
   The slanting tree.[6]

88 He hit the backs of forty tailed deer.
   He pierced the mouths and eyes of the rebels.
   He shot down three mice from the eaves,
   Were there any like him in the past?[7]

3. This took place on a hunting trip on Mount Chorae in 1372.

4. The match was held in 1356. When the ball bounced off the goal post and came back on the horse's left, Yi Sŏnggye shook off the right stirrup and turned his body in such a way that his right foot reached almost to the ground. He hit the ball cleanly, regained his mount, hit it again, and scored. The compilers called it a "sideways block."

5. An Kyŏn, a famous painter under King Sejong, painted the general's eight horses in 1446 or 1447.

6. While still young, Yi Sŏnggye shot six roebucks and six crows perched on a wall with a single arrow. During a hunt a deer escaped below a slanting tree. While the horse ran under the tree, Yi Sŏnggye vaulted over the tree, landed in the saddle on the other side, and shot the fleeing deer.

7. Yi Sŏnggye shot forty deer on a hunting trip in Haeju in 1385. During his campaign against the Mongol minister Naghacu (d. 1388) in 1362, Yi shot the rebels in the mouth.

89   Seven pinecones,
     The trunk of a dead tree,
     Three arrows piercing the helmet—
     None like him in the past.[8]

53   He opened the four borders,
     Island dwellers had no more fear of pirates.
     Southern barbarians beyond our waters,
     How could they not come to him?[9]

73   Because robbers poisoned the people,
     He initiated a land reform.
     First he drove away the usurper,
     He then labored to restore the state.[10]

76   Kind and selfless to his brothers,
     He covered their past misdeeds.
     Thus today we enjoy
     Humane manners and customs.[11]

8. To test the outcome of a battle against Japanese pirates in Hamju in 1385, Yi shot down seven pinecones with 7 arrows from 70 paces away. In 1377, before charging the Japanese pirates, Yi placed a helmet 150 paces away and divined the outcome of the campaign by hitting the target 3 times. On another occasion his arrows hit the trunk of a dead tree 3 times.

9. Yi Sŏnggye finally subjugated the Jürched in the north and the Japanese pirates in the south, and the inhabitants of even the remotest island in the south enjoyed peace. After Yi's enthronement the king of Liu-ch'iu sent an envoy to pay his respects (1392, 1394, 1397) and Siam sent an envoy with tribute (1393).

10. Yi Sŏnggye dethroned Sin Ch'ang, restored the Wang House, and set the Koryŏ dynasty in order. He also confiscated the estates monopolized by powerful families, burned the public and private land register in the ninth month of 1390, and made a new distribution of the land in 1391.

11. When his stepbrother, who plotted a revolt in 1371, was involved in a murder case, Yi did everything to help him but could not save his life (1375).

79 He was consistent from beginning to end.
Meritorious subjects were truly loyal to him.
He secured the throne for myriad years.
Would his royal works ever cease?

80 Though he was busy with war,
He loved the way of the scholar.
His work of achieving peace
Shone brilliantly.[12]

81 He did not boast of his natural gifts,
His learning was equally deep.
The vast scope of royal works
Was indeed great.[13]

82 Upon receiving an old scholar
He knelt down with due politeness.
What can you say about
His respect for scholarship?[14]

110 Your four ancestors never enjoyed peace—
How often did they move around?
How did they live,
In how large an abode?

When you live in a deep sumptuous palace,
When you enjoy golden days of peace,
Remember, my lord,
Their hardship and sorrow.

12. Yi loved learning, discussed the classics with scholars between battles, and read books far into the night.

13. Yi never boasted of his brilliant exploits. Regretting that his family had hitherto not produced a scholar, he urged his son, Yi Pangwŏn, to study the classics. The latter passed the final civil service examination in 1383.

14. When Yi Saek (1328–1396) returned from his banishment in the eleventh month of 1391, Yi Sŏnggye received him in the upper seat and kneeling down, offered him a cup.

111 Because the wolves wrought havoc,
Because not even a grass roof remained,
They bore hardships
In a clay hut.[15]

When you are in a great carpeted room,
When you sit on a richly woven throne,
Remember, my Lord,
Their hardships and sorrow.

112 Anxious only to fulfill the royal cause
He led his men from camp to camp.
How many days did he run
Without doffing his armor?[16]

When you are wrapped in a dragon robe,
When you wear the belt of precious gems,
Remember, my Lord,
His fortitude and tenacity.

113 Zealous to deliver the suffering people,
He fought on mountains and plains.
Oh, how many times did he go
Without food and drink?[17]

When you sup on northern viands and southern dainties,
When you have superb wine and precious grain,
Remember, my Lord,
His fortitude and fervor.

114 Wishing to entrust him with a great task,
Heaven flexed his bones and sinews,

15. Jürched chiefs ("wolves" in line 1) conspired against the life of Yi's great-grandfather. From canto 110 the form returns to the full two-stanza original.

16. Both verses of cantos 110–124 deal with Yi kings. While Yi was subjugating the north and the south, he never had time to remove his armor.

17. During his campaign against the Jürched and the Japanese pirates, Yi went without food for days.

And let his body suffer
Wounds and scars.[18]

While the stately guards stand row after row,
While you reign in peace and give audience,
Remember, my Lord,
His piety and constancy.

115   Because he loved men and sought their welfare,
He overawed
The fierce rebels
And caught them alive.[19]

When you have men at your beck and call,
When you punish men and sentence men,
Remember, my Lord,
His mercy and temperance.

116   Seeing the bodies lying in heaps,
He abandoned food and sleep.
Moved by love for his people,
He labored assiduously.[20]

If you are unaware of people's sorrow,
Heaven will abandon you.

18. During his campaign against the Red Turbans (1362), Yi suffered a wound below the right ear. In the 1380 campaign against the Japanese pirates, an enemy arrow hit Yi's left knee. This refers to the Confucian conception of the trials of the hero in *Mencius* 6B:15: "Heaven, when it is about to place a great burden on a man, always first tests his resolution, exhausts his frame and makes him suffer starvation and hardship, frustrates his efforts so as to shake him from his mental lassitude, toughen his nature and make good his deficiencies." D. C. Lau, *Mencius* (Hardmondsworth: Penguin, 1979), p. 181.

19. After a battle, Yi Sŏnggye returned the spoils to the people in Liaotung (1370); in his campaign against the Mongol general in 1362, Yi shot him with wooden arrows, forcing him to dismount and surrender; and in his campaign against the Japanese pirates in 1385, Yi urged his soldiers to capture them alive.

20. During his 1390 campaign against the Japanese pirates, Yi saw dead bodies piled up on the plains and hills. Overwhelmed with pity, he could neither eat nor sleep.

Remember, my Lord,
His labor of love.

117   He battled against the king's enemy,
And his fame was unrivaled.
But he never boasted of his deeds.
Such was his virtue of modesty.[21]

If a deceitful minister flatters you,
If you are roused to pride,
Remember, my Lord,
His prowess and modesty.

118   He had many to help him;
Even the Jürched served him with constancy.
How can we tell in words
The way our people gave their hearts to him?[22]

If a king loses his inward power,
Even his kin will rebel.
Remember, my Lord,
His fame and virtue.

119   The brothers rebelled against one another:
But in their heart they were friendly.
Despite their crimes
Their ties remained firm.[23]

If brothers are split,
A villain will enter and sow discord.
Remember, my Lord,
His sagacity and love.

21. The first stanza refers to the victories won by Yi Sŏnggye over the Japanese pirates in 1377, 1378, 1380, and 1385.

22. Yi enjoyed the esteem of Jürched chiefs in the northeast, and they served under his command.

23. Stanza 1 refers to the rebellion of Yi Sŏnggye's brother in 1371 and Yi Pangwŏn's elder brother in 1400.

120 Because the government burdened the people,
   The people who are Heaven to a ruler,
   He defied a multitude of opinions
   And reformed the system of private lands.

   If a ruler taxes his people without measure,
   The basis of the state will crumble.
   Remember, my Lord,
   His justice and humanity.

121 Even though they were rebellious,
   They were loyal to their lord.
   Hence he forgave them
   And employed them again.[24]

   If your advisers wrangle before you,
   Only to assist and secure the throne,
   Remember, my Lord,
   His goodness and justice.

122 His nature being one with Heaven,
   He knew learning surpassed mere thinking.
   Thus he made friends
   With learned men.[25]

   If a small man wishes to curry favor
   And preaches, "No leisure for culture,"
   Remember, my Lord,
   His effort and erudition.

123 Many slandered him;
   An innocent man was about to perish.

24. Stanza 1 refers to how the founder of the Han forgave Chi Pu, who once served the former's enemy Hsiang Yü, and how Yi Pangwŏn forgave his step-brother who rebelled in 1398.
   25. See canto 80 above.

He narrowly saved
The man of merit from death.

When slanderers craftily make mischief,
When they grossly exaggerate small mistakes.
Remember, my Lord,
His wisdom and justice.[26]

124 Because his bright nature
Was versed in the teachings of the sage,
He proscribed
Heresy.[27]

If perverse theories of the western barbarians
Threaten you with sin and allure with bliss,
Remember, my Lord,
His judgment and orthodoxy.

125 A millennium ago,
Heaven chose the north of the Han.
There they accumulated goodness and founded the state.
Oracles foretold a myriad years;
May your sons and grandsons reign unbroken.
But you can secure the dynasty only
When you worship heaven and benefit the people.
Ah, you who will wear the crown, beware.
Can you depend upon your ancestor
When you go hunting by the waters of the Lo?[28]

PL

26. Stanza 1 refers to how Yi Sŏnggye saved Cho Chun (1346–1405), who was imprisoned on a false charge (1400).

27. Stanza 1 refers to how Yi Pangwŏn upheld Confucian orthodoxy and suppressed Buddhism in 1402 by secularizing the Buddhist clergy and closing monasteries.

28. T'ai K'ang of Hsia gave himself up to pleasure and was excessively fond of hunting. Once he went to the south of the Lo River and did not return after a hundred days. I, Prince Ch'iung and a famous archer, prevented T'ai K'ang from returning to the capital and seized the throne.

SIJO

Sijo is a generic term designating a three-line lyric song (translation uses six or more lines) whose tune was standardized in the eighteenth century so that it could be sung to a uniform musical setting. Dating from the fifteenth century, the *sijo* was the most popular, elastic, and mnemonic of Korean poetic forms. Each line consists of four metric segments, with a minor pause at the end of the second segment and a major one at the end of the fourth. An emphatic syntactic division is usually introduced in the third line in the form of a countertheme, paradox, resolution, judgment, command, or exclamation introduced by characteristic phrases such as "Alas," "Let it be," "I would rather," "Why," "Truly," "I ask," and "Boy!" Often this division presents a logical and developmental transition, and a skillful poet can achieve a pattern of thought within strict formal limits and unity in variety. The introduction of a deliberate twist in phrasing or meaning is often a test of a poet's originality. Some interjections postulate a dialogue, attesting to the poet's openness to the world and his ability to inquire.

The *sijo* was sung and transmitted orally and was not written down until the early eighteenth century. The texts of most poems vary according to the source, possibly with each performance, and the great number of variants indicates the oral nature of the *sijo*. Variations range from changes in verbal endings, particles, or phrases to substitutions of whole lines. Often a single poem metamorphoses into two different poems; the more popular ones exist in numerous variants, long and short. We are not sure which *sijo* were composed during performances. In any event, the singer was free to alter phrases or lines whenever his memory failed him or his creativity inspired him. Indeed, the spoken word was the basis of his creation. The frequency of verbal parallels and formulaic expressions points to the art of creation. The poet's task was to preserve and transmit a living tradition through a new arrangement of old material, thereby imparting added significance to the tradition. The correct sequence of ideas and topics was retained in the poet's memory; he composed using phrases, motifs, and themes, each theme serving as a mnemonic device for himself and his audience. The countless variations on the same theme were a source of pleasure to members of the audience, who were quick to recognize allusions to earlier versions, to see the worth of old material in new contexts, and to savor their own aesthetic responses to the poet's creation. The fact that *sijo* were easy to sing, recite, and memorize is a good index of their popularity. A confrontation between singer and listeners constituted a dialogue between the two, and in a culture where the oral and aural coexisted with the written, the lively transmission of *sijo* is easy to imagine.

The *sijo* has proved to be a form well suited to expressing the poet's sense of the world and his response to situations in life. It is a form evolved to express one's view of the world—rather than a mutual accommodation between the two—in a simple but sensitive way. Indeed, in a well-wrought *sijo* one never feels that an emotion suffers the constriction of form. Topics include praise of the Confucian statesmen and martyrs, exemplars of social virtues, or recluses and enlightened Taoists and Buddhists. The favorite subjects of the literati are the pleasures of rural retirement and the acceptance of solitude as the only dramatic resolution of the perennial conflict between society and individual. Explorations of the relative value of the active and the contemplative, therefore, are common. Love as a subject encompasses its definition, physical symptoms, dilemmas, love as dream, metamorphosis in dream, or love after death. Most *sijo* are written in a retrospective stance with an emphasis on parting, desertion, separation, neglect, and the defeat of love by time. Poems on friendship concern parting, longing for the absent friend, celebration of a reunion with wine, moon, flowers, and music. Among the *sijo* on the topic of time, one finds acceptance of the process of time with the emblem of the falling and dying flower, poetic contemplation of the past, the notion "seize the day," and the Taoist concepts of nondiscrimination, the utility of inutility, and nonaction.

U T'AK (1262–1342)

The wind that melted the spring hills
    came and went without trace.
I wish I could bring it back
    and blow it over my head.
Would I could melt the white hair
    grown under my ears.

***

Sticks in one hand,
    brambles in the other,
I try to block old age with thorn bushes,
    and white hair with sticks.
But white hair came by a shortcut,
    having seen through my devices.

YI CHONYŎN (1269–1343)

The moon is white on pear blossoms,
    and the Milky Way tells the third watch.
A cuckoo would not know
    the intent of a branch of spring.
Too much awareness is a sickness,
    it keeps me awake all night.

YI SAEK (1328–1396)

Rough clouds gather around the valley
    where the snow still lies.
Where is the welcoming plum,
    at what place does it bloom?
I have lost my way, alone,
    in the setting sun.

PL

CHŎNG MONGJU (1337–1392)

Though this frame should die and die,
    though I die a hundred times,
My bleached bones all turn to dust,
    my very soul exist or not—
What can change the undivided heart
    that glows with faith toward my lord?

RR

YI CHONO (1341–1371)

That clouds have no intent
    is perhaps false and unreliable.
Floating in midair,
    freely moving,
For what reason do they cover
    the bright light of day?

KIL CHAE (1353–1419)

I return on horseback
    to the capital of five hundred years.
Hills and rivers remain the same,
    but where are the great men of the past?
Alas, the age of grand peace—
    it was only a dream!

WŎN CH'ŎNSŎK (C. 1401–1410)

Fortune determines rise and fall,
    Full Moon Terrace is autumn grass.
A shepherd's pipe echoes
    the royal works of five hundred years.
A traveler cannot keep back his tears
    in the setting sun.

MAENG SASŎNG (1360–1438)

Four Seasons by the Rivers and Lakes

1   Spring comes to rivers and lakes,
     wild rapture seizes me.
I drink thick wine by the river
     with a damask-scaled fish.
I can enjoy a leisurely life
     because of royal favor.

2   Summer comes to rivers and lakes,
     I am idle at the grass hut.
Friendly waves in the river
     only send a cool breeze.
I can keep myself cool
     because of royal favor.

3   Autumn comes to rivers and lakes,
     every fish is sleek.
I cast a net from my boat
     and leave it to the stream's flow.
I can while away my time
     because of royal favor.

4   Winter comes to rivers and lakes,
     snow is a foot deep.
A bamboo hat aslant,
     a straw cape for cloth,
I am not cold
     because of royal favor.

HWANG HŬI (1363–1452)

Are chestnuts falling
    in the valley of red jujubes?
And crabs crawling in the stubble
    after a harvest of rice?
Wine is ripe, and a sieve seller passes by.
    What can I do but strain and drink?

YI KAE (1417–1456)

The candle burns in the room,
    for whom has it parted?
Shedding tears outside,
    does it know that its inside burns?
That candle is like me,
    it does not know its heart burns!

SŎNG SAMMUN (1418–1456)

Were you to ask me what I'd wish to be
    after my death,
I would answer, a pine tree, tall and hardy
    on the highest peak of Mount Pongnae,
And to be green, alone, green,
    when snow fills heaven and earth.

YU ŬNGBU (D. 1456)

Do you say the wind blew last night
    and frost and snow fell?
Tall drooping pines
    are bent and broken.
What about the flower buds, then,
    what is their fate?

KING SŎNGJONG (R. 1469–1494)

Stay:
    will you go? Must you go?
Is it in weariness you go? From disgust?
    Who advised you, who persuaded you?
Say why you are leaving,
    you, who are breaking my heart.

KIM KU (1488–1534)

Until the duck's short legs
    grow as long as the crane's—
Until the crow has become white,
    white as the white heron—
Enjoy enduring bliss
    forever.

SŎ KYŎNGDŎK (1489–1546)

My mind is foolish,
    all that I do seems in vain.
Who would come to the deep mountain
    with its thick clouds, fold upon fold?
I look to see whether you come by chance,
    whenever the fallen leaves rustle in the wind.

SONG SUN (1493–1583)

I have spent ten years
    building a grass hut;
Now winds occupy half,
    the moon fills the rest.
I cannot let in hills and waters:
    I will display them all around.

***

I discuss with my heart
    whether to retire from court.
My heart scorns the intent:
    "How could you leave the king?"
"Heart, stay here and serve him,
    my old body must go."

***

Do not grieve, little birds,
    over the falling blossoms:
They're not to blame, it's the wind
    who loosens and scatters the petals.
Spring persists in leaving us,
    don't hold it against her.

CHO SIK (1501–1572)

Wearing hemp clothes in the coldest winter,
    wet with rain and snow in the cave,
I have not had the sun,
    hidden by the clouds.
But, yet, to see the setting sun
    brings tears to my eyes.

PL

YI HWANG (1501–1571)

Twelve Songs of Tosan

1 What matter if I grow like this,
    what matter if I grow like that?
What matter if I'm called
    a rustic bore?
What on earth can cure this craving
    for boulders and springs?

2 Let my house be mist and haze,
    and my friends the wind and moon;
While the land is at peace
    I'll decline into old age.
Just one thing I ask of life:
    that my faults may disappear.

3 If they say that grace is gone,
    then they surely speak a lie.
If they say human nature is noble,
    then they surely tell the truth.
Could it be that so many clever men
    have been so much deceived?

4 The orchids in the valley
    breathe a fragrance in the air,
The white clouds on the mountains
    offer wonder to the eyes—
In a place like this it is impossible
    to forget the one I serve.

5   The terrace fronts the mountain,
        the water flows below:
    Thick flocks of gulls
        wheel to and fro in the air.
    Why, oh why, glossy white colt,
        is your heart set far away?[1]

6   Springtime flowers fill the mountains,
        the autumn moon floods the terrace,
    The joys of the year are
        the stuff of life itself.
    Moreover: fish leap, kites soar, clouds pass,
        and the sun shines:
        Shall they never have an end?[2]

7   Back at the High Cloud Terrace
        my study is bright and clean.
    A lifetime of books
        has meant delights without end.
    What words can I find to describe
        delights of leisurely walks?

8   The thunder can split the mountain,
        the deaf man cannot hear;
    The noon sun can burn white in mid-heaven,
        the blind man still will not see.
    Men like us, keen-eared, clear-eyed healthy males,
        should not be like the deaf and blind.

9   The men of old never saw me,
        I never saw the men of old.
    Though I never saw the men of old,
        the paths they trod still stretch ahead.

1. Glossy white colt: reference to the *Book of Songs* 186, the mount of an honored guest, here taken as sharing his master's anxiety to leave.
2. *Book of Songs* 238. Arthur Waley, *The Book of Songs* (London: Allen and Unwin, 1954), p. 213. The self-contentedness of birds and fish.

If the paths they trod still stretch ahead,
　　should I not tread them too?

10　Many years have slipped by since
　　　I left the path I used to tread.
For awhile I went elsewhere,
　　but at last I have returned.
And now that I have come back,
　　my heart shall never roam again.

11　The green hills—how can it be
　　that they are green eternally?
Flowing streams—how can it be—
　　night and day do they never stand still?
We also, we can never stop,
　　we shall grow green eternally.

12　Even fools can know and can do.
　　Is it not easy then?
Yet even sages cannot know all.
　　Is it not difficult then?
Pondering whether it's easy or hard
　　makes me forget I grow old.

RR

HWANG CHINI (C. 1506–1544)

I will break the back
    of this long, midwinter night,
folding it double,
    cold beneath my spring quilt,
that I may draw out
    the night, should my love return.

D M

***

Do not boast of your speed,
    O blue-green stream running by the hills:
Once you have reached the wide ocean,
    you can return no more.
Why not stay here and rest,
    when Bright Moon fills the empty hills?

***

Mountains are steadfast,
    but waters are not so.
Since they flow day and night,
    can there be old waters?
Great heroes are like waters,
    once gone, they never return.

***

Blue mountains speak of my desire,
    green waters reflect my lover's love:
Green waters may flow away,
    but can blue mountains change?
Green waters too cannot forget blue mountains,
    They wander through in tears.

***

When was I unfaithful to you?
    When did I ever deceive you?
The moon sinks, and it's the third watch;
    there is no sign of you.
What can I do about
    the falling leaves in the autumn wind?

PL

***

Ah, what have I done?
Did I not know I'd miss him so?
Had I bid him stay, would he have gone?
But I did it:
I sent him away, and I can't tell you how I miss him.

OR

KWŎN HOMUN (1532–1587)

Nature makes clear the windy air
    and bright the round moon.
In the bamboo garden, on the
    pine fence, not a speck of dust.
How fresh and clean my life
    with a long lute and piled scrolls!

SŎNG HON (1535–1598)

The mountain is silent,
    the water without form.
A clear breeze has no price,
    the bright moon no lover.
Here, after their fashion,
    I will grow old in peace.

YI I (1536–1584)

Nine Songs of Mount Ko

Mount Ko's nine-bend pool
    is not yet known to people.
I weed and weave a grass hut,
    and my friends all come.
I fancy I am on Mount Wu-i[3]
    and will study Master Chu.[4]

***

Where is the first bend?
    The sun shines on the Crown Rock,
Mist clears above the tall grass,
    distant hills are a picture.
I wait for friends
    with a green goblet among the pines.

***

Where is the second bend?
    by the Flower Rock in late spring.
There let the green waves bear away
    the blossoms to the distant fields.
People do not know this superb place,
    why not tell them of this site?

3. In Fukien, China.

4. Chu Hsi (1130–1200), a Sung philosopher, generally considered the great synthesizer of neo-Confucianism.

***

Where is the third bend?
　　Where leaves cover the Emerald Screen.
Birds alight by the green water
　　and sing notes, high and low.
Twisted pines brave a clear breeze,
　　and summer's scenery is gone.

***

Where is the fourth bend?
　　The sun crosses the Pine Cliff.
Rocks swim in the water's bosom
　　reflect many hues.
Trees and springs are deep and clear—
　　I cannot suppress my joy.

***

Where is the fifth bend?
　　Hidden Screens are lovely to view.
My study by the water,
　　how cool and clean!
Here I will discuss learning
　　and make poems of moon and breeze.

***

Where is the sixth bend?
　　Fisher's Gorge has broad waters.
There I and fish delight:
　　who has a greater joy?
At twilight I walk homeward,
　　a rod on my shoulder and the moon above.

***

Where is the seventh bend?
    Autumn tints are lovely at Maple Rock.
A coat of thin clear frost
    embroiders the hanging cliffs.
Alone I sit on the cold stone
    and forget to return home.

***

Where is the eighth bend?
    The moon shines brightly on the Zither Shoal.
There I shall play on the zither
    with jade plectrums and a gold bridge.
Nobody knows the old tunes:
    I enjoy them alone.

***

Where is the ninth bend?
    The sun sets above Mount Mun.
Snow falls thick and covers over
    the rugged rocks and strange stones.
Nobody comes here for pleasure now,
    they say there is nothing to see!

CHŎNG CH'ŎL (1537–1594)

The juice of bitter herbs has
    more taste than any meat.
My small grass hut is
    a fitting abode for me.
But my longing for my lord
    chokes me with grief.

***

A dash of rain upon
    the lotus leaves. But the leaves
Remain unmarked, no matter
    how hard the raindrops beat.
Mind, be like the lotus leaves,
    unstained by the world.

***

Let forty thousand pecks of pearls
    rest on the lotus leaves.
I box and measure them
    to send them off somewhere.
Tumultuous rolling drops—
    how zestful, graceful.

***

Boys have gone out to gather bracken;
    the bamboo grove is empty.
Who will pick up the dice
    scattered on the checkerboard?
Drunk, I lean on the pine trunk,
    let dawn pass me by.

***

Milky rain on the green hills,
    can you deceive me?
Sedge cape and horsehair hat,
    can you deceive me?
Yesterday I flung off my silk robe—
    I have nothing left that will stain me.

CHO HŎN (1544–1592)

Rain sprinkles on the pond,
    smoke trails on the willows.
The boatman is gone,
    an empty boat moored to the bank.
A mateless gull comes and goes
    in the evening sun.

P L

YI SUNSIN (1545–1598)

By moonlight I sit all alone
    in the lookout on Hansan isle.
My sword is on my thigh,
    I am submerged in deep despair.
From somewhere the shrill note of a pipe
    will it sever my heartstrings?

RR

IM CHE (1549–1587)

In a mound where the grass grows long,
    are you sleeping or lying at rest?
Where is your lovely face?
    Only bones are buried here.
I have no one to offer a cup,
    and that makes me sad.

***

Deep among the green valley grasses,
    a stream runs crying.
Where's the terrace of songs,
    where's the hall of dancing?
Do you know, swallow,
    cutting the sunset water?

CHO CHONSŎNG (1553–1627)

Four Songs Calling a Boy

1   Boy, gather your straw basket,
      the sun sets on the western hills.
The fern that grew last night
      may be already withered.
What should I eat in morning and evening
      if there are no fiddleheads?

2   Boy, bring my sedge cape and bamboo hat,
      it rains at the eastern torrent.
With a long fishing rod
      and barbless hook I go.
Fishes, don't be startled!
      I came here in high spirits.

3   Boy, bring my morning porridge,
      much work to be done in the southern field.
Who will help me to work
      my clumsy plowing?
Let it be, we can plow in peace
      because of royal favor.

4   Boy, lead a cow to the northern village,
      let's taste new wine.
My face is rosy with drink,
      I'll return on cow-back in the moonlight.

> Hurrah, I am a Fu Hsi[5] tonight,
> > ancient glories at my fingertips.

5. A Chinese cultural hero, inventor of nets for hunting and fishing, writing, musical instruments, and divination through the Eight Trigrams. See Ann Birrell, *Chinese Mythology: An Introduction* (Baltimore: Johns Hopkins University Press, 1993), pp. 44–47.

HANU (DATES UNKNOWN)

Some said the northern window was bright,
    so I started out without rain gear.
But it snows in the mountain,
    and cold rain falls in the field.
Today I am wet with cold rain,[6]
    so I wish to freeze to sleep.

***

Why should you freeze to sleep?
    for what reason should you be cold?
A pillow with mandarin-duck design and
    kingfisher-pattern quilt,
how could you freeze tonight?
Since you came, wet with cold rain,
    won't you melt in bed with me?

6. The name of this female entertainer Hanu means "cold rain," hence the pun in this and the next songs.

HONGNANG (FL. 1576–1600)

I send you, my love,
    select branches of the willow.
Plant them to be admired
    outside your bedroom window.
If a night rain makes them bud,
    think that it is I.

KYERANG (YI HYANGGŬM, 1513–1550)

Under a shower of pear blossoms
    we parted in tears, clinging to each other.
Now autumn winds scatter leaves,
    are you too thinking of me?
A thousand miles away,
    only my lonely dreams come and go.

MYŎNGOK (LATE SIXTEENTH CENTURY)

They say dream visits
    are "only a dream."
My longing to see him is destroying me.
    Where else do I see him but in dreams?
Darling, come to me even if it be in dreams.
    Let me see you time and again.

***

Snow falls on the mountain village
    and buries the stone path.
Do not open the twig gate,
    who will come to visit me here?
My only friend is
    a slice of bright moon.

CH'ŎN KŬM (DATES UNKNOWN)

Night draws near in a mountain village,
    a dog barks far away.
I open the twig gate:
    the chilly sky and the moon.
Be still, stop barking at the moon
    asleep over the bare mountain.

KIM SANGYONG (1561–1637)

Listlessly I hear the rain
    beat on the paulownia's wide leaves.
My grief awakes, and every raindrop
    on the leaves brings sorrow.
Never again shall I plant
    a tree with such broad leaves.

***

Love is a deceit.
    She does not love me.
She says she comes to me in a dream:
    it is a lie.
Lying awake every night,
    in what dream shall I see her?

SIN HŬM (1566–1628)

I would draw her face with blood
    that lies stagnant in my heart.
And on the plain wall of a high hall,
    I would hang it up to gaze.
Who has invented the word *Farewell?*
    Who causes me to die?

***

A rain came overnight;
    pomegranates are in full bloom.
Having rolled up a crystal screen
    by the lotus pond,
Can I unravel this deep sorrow—
    caused by someone I love?

***

Don't laugh if my roof beams
    are long or short, the pillars
Tilted or crooked, or my grass hut small.
    Moonlight that pours on the vines,
The encircling hills,
    are mine—and mine alone.

***

The person who made a song
    must have had many sorrows.
Unable to say what he wanted,
    he must have sung it.
If song could dispel sorrow,
    I too will start to sing.

KIM YUK (1580–1658)

Be sure to invite me
        when your wine matures.
I shall invite you
        if flowers bloom in my arbor.
We shall discuss, then, how to live
        a hundred years without worry.

KIM KWANGUK (1580–1656)

Have you seen a person
    who returned from death?
None ever told us he came back,
    no one has seen another return.
Since I know this is so,
    I'll savor life's joys.

***

Bamboo stick, the sight of you
    fills me with trust and delight.
Ah, boyhood days when you were my horse!
    Stand there now
behind the window, and when we go out,
    let me stand behind you.

***

Bundle the piles of verbose missives
    and throw them away!
At last I ride home on a swift horse
    whipping the autumn winds.
No bird freed could be happier.
    What freedom, what relief!

YUN SŎNDO (1587–1671)

Songs of Five Friends

How many friends have I? Count them:
    water and stone, pine and bamboo—
The rising moon on the east mountain,
    welcome. It too is my friend.
What need is there, I say,
    to have more friends than five?

***

They say the color of clouds is fine,
    but they often darken.
They say the sound of winds is clear,
    but they often cease to blow.
It is only the *water*, then,
    that is perpetual and good.

***

Why do flowers fade so soon
    once they are in their glory?
Why do grasses yellow so soon
    once they have grown tall?
Perhaps it is the *stone*, then,
    that is constant and good.

***

Flowers bloom when it is warm;
    leaves fall when the days are cool.
But, O *pine*, how is it
    that you scorn frost, ignore snow?
I know now even your roots are
    straight among the Nine Springs.[7]

***

You are not a tree,
    nor are you a plant.
Who let you shoot up so straight?
    What makes you empty within?
You are green in all seasons.
    Welcome, my friend.

***

Small but floating high,
    you shed light on all creation.
And what can match your brightness
    in the dark of night?
You see everything but say nothing;
    that's why, O *moon*, you are my friend.

7. The underworld.

The Angler's Calendar (1651)

Spring
1 Fog lifts in the stream before me,
      the sun lances the black hills.
Cast off, cast off!
The night tide neaps, and now
      high water rushes upon the shore.
Chigukch'ong chigukch'ong ŏsawa.[8]
Flowers in river hamlets are fair to see,
      but distant views swell my heart.

2 Day is warm,
      fishes float in the blue.
Hoist anchor, hoist anchor!
In twos or threes,
      gulls come and go.
Chigukch'ong chigukch'ong ŏsawa.
Boy, I have a rod;
      have you loaded a flagon of wine?

3 A puff of east wind ruffles
      the stream's surface into ripples.
Raise sail, raise sail!
Let's go to West Lake
      by the East.
Chigukch'ong chigukch'ong ŏsawa.

8. Three three-syllable onomatopoeic words imitate the sound of the oars.

Hills pass by,
>more hills greet us.

4   Is it a cuckoo that cries?
>Is it the willow that is blue?
Row away, row away!
Several roofs in a far fishing village
>swim in the mist.
Chigukch'ong chigukch'ong ŏsawa.
Boy, fetch an old net!
>Fishes are climbing against the stream.[9]

5   The sun's fair rays are shining.
>Water shimmers like oil.
Row away, row away!
Should we cast a net,
>or drop a line on such a day?
Chigukch'ong chigukch'ong ŏsawa.
The Fisherman's Song stirs my fancy;[10]
>I have forgotten all about fishing.

6   Let's return to the shore,
>twilight trails in the west.
Lower sail, lower sail!
How supple and sweet
>willows and flowers on the riverbank!
Chigukch'ong chigukch'ong ŏsawa.
Who would envy three dukes?
>Who would now think of earthly affairs?

7   Let's tread on fragrant grasses
>and pick orchids and angelica.
Stop the boat, stop the boat!

9. Another version of lines 7–8 reads: "In the deep and clear stream, / All kinds of fish are leaping." See Sim Chaewan, *Kyobon yŏktae sijo chŏnsŏ* [Variorum edition of the complete canon of sijo] (Seoul: Sejong munhwasa, 1972), no. 2176, pp. 770–772.
10. This refers to "The Fisherman" in *Elegies of Ch'u (Ch'u Tz'u).*

What have I taken aboard
    on my boat small as a leaf ?
Chigukch'ong chigukch'ong ŏsawa.
Nothing except mist when I set sail,
    when I row back, the moon.

8   Drunk I lie asleep,
    what if the boat floats downstream?
Moor the boat, moor the boat!
Peach Blossom Spring is near,[11]
    pink petals leap on the stream.
Chigukch'ong chigukch'ong ŏsawa.
I am far away from red dust—
    the world of men.

9   Let's stop angling and see
    the moon through the bamboo awning.
Drop anchor, drop anchor!
Night settles,
    the cuckoo sings a sweet song.
Chigukch'ong chigukch'ong ŏsawa.
The heart shouts its peak of joy,
    I have lost my way in the dark.

10   Tomorrow, tomorrow, we have tomorrow.
    A spring night will soon see the day.
Bring the boat ashore, bring the boat ashore!
With a rod for a cane,
    let's find our twig gate.
Chigukch'ong chigukch'ong ŏsawa.
This angler's life is
    how I shall pass my days.

11. The first Chinese ideal place (*locus amoenus*) created by the poet T'ao Ch'ien (365–427), for which see James R. Hightower, *The Poetry of T'ao Ch'ien* (Oxford: Clarendon, 1970), pp. 254–258.

Summer

11   Tedious rain over at last,
        the stream grows limpid.
Cast off, cast off!
Rod on my shoulder,
        I can't still my loud heart.
Chigukch'ong chigukch'ong ŏsawa.
Who has painted these scenes,
        misty rivers and folded peaks?

12   Wrap the steamed rice in lotus leaves,
        you need no other viands.
Hoist anchor, hoist anchor!
I've already got my blue arum hat,
        bring me, boy, my green straw cape.
Chigukch'ong chigukch'ong ŏsawa.
Mindless gulls come and go;
        do they follow me, or I them?

13   A wind rises among the water chestnut,
        cool is the bamboo awning.
Raise sail, raise sail!
Let the boat drift with the current,
        the summer breeze is capricious.
Chigukch'ong chigukch'ong ŏsawa.
Northern coves and southern river,
        does it matter where I go?

14   When the river is muddy,
        no matter if we wash our feet there.
Row away, row away!
I wish to go to the Wu River; sad
        are the angry waves of a thousand years.[12]
Chigukch'ong chigukch'ong ŏsawa.

12. Lines 4–5 refer to Wu Yuan, a native of Ch'u. Denounced by Fu Ch'ai (r. 495–473), king of Wu, he committed suicide. Fu was angry and caused his body to be put in a leather sack and thrown into the Wu River; on the bank the people raised a shrine to his memory. *Shih chi* (Peking: Chunghua, 1974) 66:2180.

Paddle the boat, then, to the Ch'u River;[13]
but don't catch the fish of a loyal soul.

15   How rare is a mossy jetty
         with willow groves, thick and green.
Row away, row away!
Remember when we reach the fishing rock,
         anglers don't fight for the best pool.
Chigukch'ong chigukch'ong ŏsawa.
When you meet a hoary hermit,
         yield him the choicest stream.[14]

16   Whelmed by my exalted mood,
         I had not known day was ending.
Lower sail, lower sail!
Let's beat the stroke
         with a song of roving waves.
Chigukch'ong chigukch'ong ŏsawa.
Who can know how my heart
         always delights in the creak of an oar?

17   The setting sun is splendid.
         Twilight will soon overtake us!
Stop the boat, stop the boat!
Under the pine a path
         winds through the rocks.
Chigukch'ong chigukch'ong ŏsawa.
Do you hear an oriole calling
         here and there in the green grove?

18   Let's spread our net out on the sand
         and lie under the thatched awning.

13. Lines 7–8 refer to Ch'ü Yüan (c. 343–278 B.C.), who drowned himself in
the Milo (or Ch'u) River. See *Shih chi* 84:2481–2491; Burton Watson, *Records of the
Grand Historian of China*, 2 vols. (New York: Columbia University Press, 1961)
1:499–508, especially p. 507.
14. Refers to a tradition that when the Emperor Shun went to Mount Li he
was given a field, and when he went to Lei Stream he was given a good place for
fishing. *Shih chi* 1:33–34.

Moor the boat, moor the boat!
Fan off mosquitoes,
    no, flies are worse.
Chigukch'ong chigukch'ong ŏsawa.
Only one worry: even here,
    traitors might eavesdrop.[15]

19 What will the mood of the sky be?
    Winds and storm may rise at night.
Drop anchor, drop anchor!
Who said that a boat swings by itself
    at the ferry landing?[16]
Chigukch'ong chigukch'ong ŏsawa.
Lovely are the hidden plants
    growing along mountain torrents.

20 Look! My snail-shell hut
    with white clouds all around.
Bring the boat ashore, bring the boat ashore!
Let's climb the stone path
    with bulrush fan in hand.
Chigukch'ong chigukch'ong ŏsawa.
O idle life of an old angler,
    this is my work, this is my life.

Autumn

21 What is more transcendent
    than the life of a complete angler?
Cast off, cast off!
Mock not a hoary fisherman;
    he's painted by every great hand.
Chigukch'ong chigukch'ong ŏsawa.

15. Minister Sang in the original: Sang Hung-yang (152–180 B.C.). It is not clear why Sang is brought in to serve as a duplicitous courtier here. For Sang see *Shih chi* 30:1428–1442.

16. Lines 4–5 refer to Wei Ying-wu (b. 736), "West Creek at Ch'u-chou"; see Burton Watson, *The Columbia Book of Chinese Poetry: From Early Times to the Thirteenth Century* (New York: Columbia University Press, 1984), p. 278.

Are the joys of all seasons equal?
    No, autumn has the most delights.

22 Autumn comes to a river village,
    the fishes are many and sleek.
Hoist anchor, hoist anchor!
Let's be free and happy
    on myriad acres of limpid waves.
Chigukch'ong chigukch'ong ŏsawa.
Behind me the dusty world, but
    joy doubles as I sail farther way.

23 Where white clouds rise,
    branches rustle.
Raise sail, raise sail!
Let's go to West Lake at high tide,
    and at low water to East Lake.
Chigukch'ong chigukch'ong ŏsawa.
White clover ferns and pink knotweeds—
    they adorn every inlet.

24 Beyond where the wild geese fly
    unknown peaks emerge.
Row away, row away!
I'll angle there, of course, but
    my zestful spirit is enough.
Chigukch'ong chigukch'ong ŏsawa.
As the setting sun shines,
    a thousand hills are brocade.

25 Silver scales and jade scales,
    did I have a good catch today?
Row away, row away!
Let's build a fire of reed bushes,
    broil the fishes one by one.
Chigukch'ong chigukch'ong ŏsawa.
Pour wine from a crock jar
    filling up my gourd cup!

26   Gently, the side wind blowing,
         we return with sail lowered.
     Lower sail, lower sail!
     Darkness is overcoming the day,
         but clear delight lingers.
     Chigukch'ong chigukch'ong ŏsawa.
     Who can tire of
         the red trees and crystal waters?

27   A scatter of silver dews;
         the bright moon rises.
     Stop the boat, stop the boat!
     Far and foggy is the Phoenix Tower,[17]
         to whom should I give this clear light?
     Chigukch'ong chigukch'ong ŏsawa.
     The jade hare pounds the magic pills;
         would I could feed them to heroes.

28   Where is it, where am I?
         Are heaven and earth separate?
     Moor the boat, moor the boat!
     Since the west wind's dust can't reach us,
         why fan off the empty air?[18]
     Chigukch'ong chigukch'ong ŏsawa.
     Further, since I have heard no words,
         why should I bother to wash my ears?[19]

29   Frost falls on my clothes:
         I am not cold.

17. The Phoenix Tower is the palace. In East Asian mythology the rabbit is pounding magic medicine in the moon.

18. In their struggles for power, Wang Tao (276–339) referred to Yü Liang (289–340) as being filthy as dust. The wind is a "west wind," probably because Yü Liang served as General Chastizing the West. "A strong wind started to raise the dust, and Wang [Tao], whisking it away with his fan, said 'Yü Liang's dust is contaminating me!" See Richard B. Mather, trans., *A New Account of Tales of the World* (Minneapolis: University of Minnesota Press, 1976), p. 429.

19. When the sage-king Yao wished to make the recluse Hsü Yu his successor, Hsü went to the Ying River to wash his ears.

Drop anchor, drop anchor!
Don't complain that the boat is narrow;
    compare it instead to the floating world.
Chigukch'ong chigukch'ong ŏsawa.
We'll live this way
    tomorrow and ever.

30 I want to admire the dawn moon
    from a stone cave in the pine grove.
Bring the boat ashore, bring the boat ashore!
But the path in the empty hills
    is hidden by fallen leaves.
Chigukch'ong chigukch'ong ŏsawa.
Since the white clouds, too, follow me,
    O heavy is the sedge cape!

Winter

31 The clouds have rolled away,
    the sun's rays are warm.
Cast off, cast off!
Heaven and earth are frozen hard,
    but water as always is clear and cold.
Chigukch'ong chigukch'ong ŏsawa.
The boundless water
    is silk brocade.

32 Mend your fishing line and rod,
    repair the boat with bamboo sheets.
Hoist anchor, hoist anchor!
They say the nets on the Hsiao and Hsiang
    and the Tungt'ing Lake freeze.[20]
Chigukch'ong chigukch'ong ŏsawa.
At this time no place is
    better than our waters.

20. The Hsiao and Hsiang Rivers and Tungt'ing Lake are in northeastern Hunan.

33 Fishes in the shallows
    are gone to distant swamps.
Raise sail, raise sail!
The sun shines for a moment;
    so let's go out to the fishing place.
Chigukch'ong chigukch'ong ŏsawa.
If the bait is good,
    fat fishes will bite, they say.

34 A snow settles over the night—
    what new scenes before my eyes!
Row away, row away!
In front lie glassy acres,
    jade hills piled behind.
Chigukch'ong chigukch'ong ŏsawa.
Is it a fairy land, or Buddha's realm?
    It can't be the world of man.

35 I've forgotten the net and rod
    and beat the side of the boat.
Row away, row away!
How many times have I wished
    to cross the stream ahead?
Chigukch'ong chigukch'ong ŏsawa.
What if a gale should rise
    and set my boat in motion?

36 The crows hastening to their nests,
    how many have flown overhead?
Lower sail, lower sail!
Darkness envelops our homeward path,
    evening snow lies thick.
Chigukch'ong chigukch'ong ŏsawa.
Who'll attack Oya Lake[21]

21. In 817 the T'ang general Li Su took Ts'ai-chou in Honan by surprise and captured Wu Yüan-chi (783–817). Appearing before the enemy stronghold on a snowy night, he had the wildfowl flushed from the numerous ponds outside the walls so that their noise might drown the sound of the approaching army. See *Chiu T'ang shu* (Peking: Chunghua, 1975) 133:3680; *Hsin T'ang shu* (Peking: Chunghua, 1975) 154:4877.

    and avenge the shame of soldier trees?[22]

37 Red cliffs and emerald canyons
      enfold us like a painted screen.
Stop the boat, stop the boat!
What does it matter
      if I catch any fish or not?[23]
Chigukch'ong chigukch'ong ŏsawa.
In an empty boat, with straw cape and hat,
      I sit and my heart beats fast.

38 By the river a lone pine,
      how mighty, how towering.
Moor the boat, moor the boat!
Don't scorn the rough clouds—
      they screen the world from us.
Chigukch'ong chigukch'ong ŏsawa.
Don't deplore the roaring waves—
      they drown out the clamor of this world.

39 People have praised my way of life
      in the land of the hermits.
Drop anchor, drop anchor!
Tell me who wore
      the sheepskin cloth at Seven-League Shallows?[24]

22. The king of the Former Ch'in, Fu Chien (338–385), attacked the Eastern Chin and suffered a crushing defeat in 383. The retreating army feared ambush in every tree and tuft of grass and was alarmed by the sound of the wind and the whoop of cranes. *Chin shu* (Peking: Chunghua, 1974) 114:2918.

23. The original refers to "fish with big mouths and delicate scales"; Su Shih, "The Red Cliff 2," in Burton Watson, *Su Tung-p'o* (New York: Columbia University Press, 1965), p. 91.

24. Yen Kuang (37 B.C.–A.D. 43), a contemporary of Emperor Kuang-wu, retired to Mount Fu-ch'un and spent his time fishing because he wished to decline the latter's offer of a high post. *Hou Han shu* (Peking: Chunghua, 1963) 113: 2763–2764.

Chigukch'ong chigukch'ong ŏsawa.
And for three thousand six hundred days
let's count the time on our fingers.[25]

40 Day closes,
time to feast and rest.
Bring the boat ashore, bring the boat ashore!
Let's tread the path where snow
is strewn with pink petals.
Chigukch'ong chigukch'ong ŏsawa.
Lean from the pine window and gaze
as the snow moon crosses the western peak.

25. Refers to T'ai Kung Wang or Lü Shang, a counselor to King Wen of Chou who found him fishing in the Wei River. He was the subject of poems by Li Po and Po Chü-i. See *Shih chi* 32:1477–1481.

YI MYŎNGHAN (1596–1645)

If the path of my dreams
    left footprints,
The road outside your window, even of stone,
    would have been worn down.
But no trace remains on dream paths,
    and that makes me sad.

***

With tears I cling to your sleeves,
    do not shake them and leave.
Over the far-off long dike
    the sun goes down.
You will regret it trimming the lamp
    by the tavern window without sleep.

***

The morning star has set. A lark
    rises out of the long grass as I take
My hoe and close my twig gate.
    my cloth breeches are wet with dew.
Boy, if these were peaceful times,
    who'd be fretting about his wet clothes?

PL

YI YŎNG (1615–1637)

Who sliced the crescent moon so small;
who drew the full moon so round?
Streams flow but do not dry up; smoke disappears
        as soon as it rises.
I don't understand
the waxing and waning of this world.

OR

PRINCE PONGNIM (1619–1659)

What amuses you in the sound
    of rain on the clear stream?
O flowers and trees of the hill,
    you shake and laugh?
Take pleasure, then, while you may;
    only a few more spring days.

PRINCE INP'YŎNG (1622–1658)

Don't mock a pine
    twisted and bent by the winds.
Flowers in the spring wind,
    can they keep their brilliance?
When wind blows and snow whirls,
    you will call for me.

YI T'AEK (1651–1719)

O roc, don't ridicule the small black birds:
You and the little birds both fly way up in the clouds,
You're a bird,
They're birds.
Really, I can't see much difference between you!

P L

YUN TUSŎ (B. 1668)

A mud-encrusted piece of jade
    lies abandoned by the road.
People coming, people going
    all look on it as dirt.
Stay as you are, jade stone,
    someone will recognize you for what you are.

OR

CHU ŬISIK (1675–1720)

A boy stops outside my window,
    tells me it is the New Year.
So I look out my eastern window—
    the usual sun has risen.
Boy, it's the same old sun,
    come tell me in the next world.

***

What is life, I ponder—
    it is just a dream!
All good things and bad,
    they're dreams within a dream.
If this is so, all right—
    why not enjoy this dreaming?

KIM SUJANG (B. 1690)

In my quiet grass hut,
    I sit alone.
The clouds are dozing
    to the low melody of my song.
Who else is there that can know
    the subtle intent of my life?

***

Standing in your lofty tower,
    don't laugh at this low place.
In the midst of thunder and storm,
    would you be surprised to slip?
We sit on level ground,
    who needs distinctions?

YI CHŎNGBO (1693–1766)

If flowers bloom, I think of the moon,
    if the moon shines, I ask for wine.
When I have all these at once,
    still I think of friends.
When can I drink a night away,
    enjoying moon and flowers with a friend?

CHO MYŎNGNI (1697–1756)

Wild geese have all flown away,
    the first frosts have come.
Long, long is the autumn night,
    many, many are the traveler's worries.
When moonlight floods the garden,
    I feel I am back at home.

KIM SŎNGGI (C. 1725–1776)

Shaking off the red dust,
    a bamboo stick in hand, sandals on foot,
I go into the hills and waters
    with the black zither.
I hear the whoop of a lone crane
    somewhere beyond the clouds.

KIM CH'ŎNT'AEK (C. 1725–1776)

Having given my clothes to a boy
    to have them pawned at the tavern,
Looking up to heaven,
    I question the moon.
Who is Li Po, that ancient drunkard,[26]
    what is he compared with me?

26. Know as "a transcendent banished from heaven," Li Po (701–762) is one of
the great Chinese poets known for his poems on wine.

KIM YŎNG (FL. 1776–1800)

Snowflakes flutter—butterflies chase flowers;
    ants float—my wine is thick.
I pluck the black zither,
    a crane dances to my tune.
A dog barks at the wicker gate—
    boy, see if my friend has come.

PAK HYOGWAN (C. 1850–1880)

If my lovesick dream
     became the spirit of a cricket,
In the long, long autumn night,
     it would enter my love's room
And wake her from her sleep,
     the sound sleep that has forgotten me.

***

She came to my dream,
     but was gone when I woke.
Where has she gone leaving me,
     the one I long for?
Dreams may be empty,
     but visit me as often as you can.

AN MINYŎNG (FL. 1870–1880)

Speak, chrysanthemum, why do you shun
    the orient breezes of the third moon?
"I had rather freeze in a cruel rain
    beside the hedge of dried sticks
Than humble myself to join the parade:
    those flowers of a fickle spring."

PL

ANONYMOUS

At the wind that blew last night,
    peach blossoms fell, scattered in the garden.
A boy came out with a broom,
    intending to sweep them away.
No, do not sweep them away, no, no.
    Are fallen flowers not flowers?

***

A horse neighs, wants to gallop:
    my love clings to me, begs me to stay.
The sun has crossed the hill.
    I have a thousand miles to go.
My love, do not stop me:
    stop the sun from setting!

***

The faint moon in a heavy frost;
    a solitary goose flies crying.
I fancied it brought me news.
    Was it a letter from my love?
No, I hear only the bird
    beyond the clouds, incredibly far off.

***

In the valley where the stream leaps,
    having built a grass hut by the rock,
I till the field under the moon,
    lie down among the vast clouds.
Heaven and earth advise me
    to age together with them.

***

I have lived anxious and hurt.
    Enough, I would rather die,
Become the spirit of the cuckoo
    when the moon is on the bare hills,
And sing with bitter tears
    to him my forbidden hopes.

***

What is love, what is it?
    Is it round, is it square?
Is it long, is it short?
    More than an inch, more than a yard?
It seems of no great length,
    but somehow I don't know where it ends.

***

O love, round as the watermelon,
    do not use words sweet as the melon.
What you have said, this and that,
    was all wrong, and you mocked me.
Enough, your empty talk
    is hollow, like a preserved melon.

P L

***

Girl, don't be so haughty;
don't boast of your beauty.

Have you never seen the wild chrysanthemums that bloom
    on the hill behind your house?
One touch of
Ninth- or tenth-month frost and they become kindling for the
    fire.

***

Moon, round moon, moon that shines
through my beloved's east window,
does he lie alone, or does he hold some young love
    in his arms?
Moon,
tell it as you see it; for me this is life and death.

***

One by one I've gathered up my feelings of love;
I've measured them, bagged them.
They're loaded now on the straight back of a fine strong horse.
Hey, lad,
give her the whip; send them off to my love.

***

I live at the foot of the mountain;
even the cuckoo embarrasses me.
It laughs at the size of my cooking pot when it peeks
    into my house.
Believe me, bird,
it's plenty big in terms of my interest in the world.

***

Parting turns to fire;
it burns up my innards.
Tears become rain; perhaps they'll quench that fire.
But sighs
become the wind; will the fire live or die?

OR

SASŎL SIJO

Sasŏl sijo is a form of sijo in which more than two metric segments are added in each line (except for the first in the third line). Judging from the 550 or so extant pieces, mostly by anonymous writers, the form enjoyed great popularity from the eighteenth century on. In addition to external structure, the writers introduced innovations in topic, breadth and sweep, voice, diction, point of view, and rhetorical pattern. A typical sasŏl sijo draws from colloquial speech, including taboo words and puns. A marked feature is enumeration—a list of different windows and hinges in the heart, for example, or a catalog of a woman's personal ornaments. One speaker lists as ingredients of a good life an automatically heating iron kettle, a horse, a cow, and a concubine who weaves. Often these examples are cited by scholars to illustrate the hedonistic ethos of sasŏl sijo.

Sasŏl sijo are also known for their presentation of the texture of ordinary low life—especially the explicit presentation of sex, often with exaggeration, grotesquerie, and caricature. Some poems cast a satiric glance at the corrupt, foolish, and lascivious to capture various aspects of lowly life. Others are comic variations on the topic of the lovelorn speaker's wish for a metamorphosis to achieve a union. A favorite rhetorical tactic is to begin the poem with a series of similes and mention the real subject of comparison only at the end. Enumeration gives a sense of plenitude: that the earth is full of wonders, delights, and torments. Bringing a new dimension to the form, sasŏl sijo exude worldliness and the capacity for laughter. The sound, color, and feel of words are robust and original, and these are the qualities we associate with the form at its most characteristic.

CHŎNG CH'ŎL (1537–1594)

Let's drink a cup of wine; let's drink another!
With petals from flowers we've cut, let's mark our cups; let's
    drink
      and drink, let's drink forever!
For when at last this body dies, it will be wrapped in a straw mat
    and strapped to a jiggy,[1] or, perhaps, it will be borne on an
    elegantly decked bier, ten thousand standard bearers
    shedding tears. Either way, once among the reeds and
    rushes, the oaks and willows, when the sun is yellow and
    the moon is white, when fine rain falls or thick snowflakes
    flurry, when whirlwinds blow a mournful dirge, who will
    offer me a cup?
Need I add:
when monkeys whistle on my grave, won't it be too late for
    regrets?

1. The jiggy is an A-frame, wooden carrier strapped to the bearer's back.

KIM SUJANG (B. 1690)

Moonlight shines on the lotus pond;
lotus fragrance pervades my clothes.
There's wine in the golden jug and a beauty playing the black
   zither.
      Captivated by the mood, I sing a sad refrain. Pine and
      bamboo sway to my song; the cranes in the garden
      dance.
Thus,
happy with relatives, glad with friends, I'll live the span allotted
   me
     by heaven.

***

Of all the dogs around me, spotted, black, and hairy,
that yellow bitch is certainly the most frustrating by far.
In sheer delight she runs to welcome those whom I despise,
      while
      those I like she barks at, rooting them outside.
The next dog-monger
who passes by my gate will get that bitch trussed tightly,
      abandoned
      to her fate.

OR

YI CHŎNGBO (1693–1766)

May my love become an alder tree
    of Kŭmsŏng in Hoeyang, and
    I an arrowroot vine in
    the third month or fourth:
Like a spider's web around a butterfly,
    the vine goes around the tree,
    tightly this way, tightly that,
    wrongly loosened, properly wound,
    bound, then loosened from down below
    all the way to the top,
    tightly winding round and round
    without a single gap, and
    unchanging, day and night,
    it's coiled around, twisting.
Though, in the heart of winter,
    we may bear wind, rain, snow, and frost,
    could we ever be apart?

***

When the owl hoots,
    atop yonder Wŏrang Rock,
    in the middle of each night:
"Those of old have said,
    the young concubine who,
    hateful and detestable,
    becomes someone's paramour, and
    lures him with her

cunning wiles, is cursed to
die a sudden death!"
The concubine replies,
    "O honored wife, do not speak
    such delirious words:
    it's the old wife, who
    mistreats her lord, and is
    so very jealous of the
    concubine, who dies first,
    I've heard them say."

W H

***

I'll never forget the boy
who slept here last night.
He could be the son of a tile-maker the way clay yields to
    his touch, or the scion of a mole, the way he burrows
    and thrusts, or perhaps the stripling of a seaman, the
    way the oar answers his pulse. His first experience, he
    avows, a claim that raises certain doubts.
I've had my share
before and I assume I'll have some more, but the memory of
    that boy last night is a pleasure I shall always store.

O R

ANONYMOUS

Like a hen pheasant
    chased by a hawk
    on a treeless, rockless mountain.
Like a ship captain on the high seas,
    his cargo a thousand bags of grain,
    oars and anchor lost,
    rigging broken,
    sail torn,
    rudder gone,
    wind howling, waves billowing,
    endless miles to go under a foggy sky,
    darkness on all sides,
    heaven and earth desolate,
    and then to be robbed by pirates.
To what can I liken my sorrow
    when you left me two days ago?

***

Pass where the winds pause before they cross,
    pass where the clouds pause before they cross,
the pass of Changsŏng ridge
    where wild-born falcons,
    tamed falcons,
    peregrine falcons,
    and yearling falcons pause before they cross—
If they said my love were over the pass,
I would cross it without a pause.

***

Take apart your cassock and make a coat,
    unstring your rosary to make a donkey's crupper.
After ten years of studying
    the realm of Śākyamuni,
    the Pure Land of bliss,
    the bodhisattva Sound Observer,
    and "I put my faith in Amitābha,"
    now you go away.
At night in a nun's bosom,
    you've no time to invoke the Buddha!

***

Middle- and small-sized needles
    dropped in the midst of the sea.
They say with a foot-long pole
    a dozen boatmen hooked the eye of every needle and pulled
    them up.
Love, my love,
    don't swallow everything you hear
    when they tell you a hundred tales.

***

You, wild hawk,
stop rending my innards.
Shall I give you money?
Shall I give you silver?
    A Chinese silk skirt,
    a Korean ritual dress,
    gauze petticoats,
    white satin belt,
    a cloudy wig from the north,
    a jade hairpin,
    a bamboo hairpin,
    a silk knife in an inlaid case,
    a golden knife in an amber case,

a coral brooch from the far south,
a gold ring set with a blue bell
shaped like a heavenly peach,
sandals with yellow pearl strings,
embroidered hemp sandals?
For a night worth thousands of gold pieces,
give me one chance at your dimples,
lovely and fresh as a flower,
grant me only one night,
priceless as a swift steed!

PL

***

Sigh, O thin sigh, through
    what crack have you entered?
With a sliding screen,
    a thin-framed screen, and
    other sliding doors,
    a hinge on the sidepost, and,
    on the door, a latch fastened with a
    clang, a lock, fastened firmly, of
    dragon and turtle design,
    a hinged screen folded with a
    clatter, a scroll rolled
    tightly up, through what
    crack could you have entered?
Somehow, on nights when
    you come, I cannot sleep.

***

Why could you not come? For what reason
    could you not come?
On your way, did they build a fortress of
    cast iron, a wall within the fortress, and
    a house within the wall, then did they put
    a chest within the house, a box within
    the chest, and bind you in the box,

locking it firmly with a lock, of
    dragon and turtle design, on a double bolt?
    Why do you not come?
There are thirty days in a month, will there
    not be one day you come to me?

***

Mother-in-law, do not stamp
    on the kitchen floor
    for hatred of your
    daughter-in-law!
Was she payment for a debt,
    was she bought for a price?
    Father-in-law, severe as a sprig
    from the rotting stump of
    a chestnut tree,
    Mother-in-law, shriveled as
    sun-baked cattle dung,
    Sister-in-law, sharp as
    a new gimlet poking from a straw bag
    woven three years ago, and—
    like a poor crop on a field
    that's made for planting good grain,
    having borne a son like
    a bright yellow cucumber flower,
    who has the bloody flux,
Daughter-in-law, like the bindweed
    on a fertile field:
    why do they hate her so?

***

Listen to me, you wench!
When you first saw me, you said
    you'd stay with me forever:
    firmly believing in your words
    I sold my house, the land around,
    my oven and my kettle,

my horse with a coat of deep ebony,
good rice fields, and even my black cow—
didn't I then give all to you?
For what reason, who has done you wrong,
that you amuse yourself with another?

My love, if you too have deceived me,
would I not deceive you?

***

When on a cold day with deep snow,
I seek my love, climbing
toward the very heavens:
I take off my shoes to
clutch in my hand,
my socks to hold in my arms, then
helter-skelter,
scurrying, hurrying,
without a moment's rest,
I struggle up panting, and
Yet, though my unshod feet
do not smart with cold,
my heart, under my
tightened collar, chills me.

***

I loathe them, I loathe them,
I loathe great mansions high above,
Slaves and farms, silken gowns,
silken skirts, violet silk jackets,
knives of amber, braided hair, and
precious mineral dyes are all,
all but the stuff of dreams!
He for whom I wish is a true gallant
upon a white steed with a golden whip,
of great height and fair of face,
a scholar, an orator,

a singer, a dancer,
an archer, a chess master, and,
what's more, a gentle lover.

WH

***

A blind man carried
a blind man on his back.
Without supports on his clogs, or stockings on his feet, or a stick
    in his hand, he inched across a rotten single-log bridge.
A stone Buddha,
 standing beneath, guffawed at the sky.

***

People, kind people, please buy my powder and rouge.
Vendor, good vendor, I'll buy, if your wares are fine.
How fine my wares are I cannot say, but once rubbed on,
    you'll have an allure you hadn't before.
If your claims,
vendor, are true, five, six large measures is what I'll buy,
    even if I have to sell my old underwear.

***

A toad grabbed a fly in its mouth
and hopped on top of a compost pile.
It looked across at the mountain opposite, and saw a peregrine
    falcon hovering in flight. The toad shuddered, started,
    tumbled from atop the compost pile.
Fortunately the toad
was exceptionally agile, otherwise severe contusions would have
    been
its lot.

***

My love is coming! I take dinner early,
 run out the middle gate, to the outside gate, and sit on the
   step. I shield my eyes with my hand. Is he coming or
   not? I look at the mountain opposite. Something black
   and white is standing there: it must be my love.
Stockings clutched to my breast, shoes in my hand, I begin to
   run,
   racing, rolling, faster, still faster, oblivious of dry ground or
   wet—for I have words of love to say. One quick look tells
   me all: last year's stripped flax stalks have deceived me.
Luckily
it is night, for if it were day, I might be the laughingstock of the
   place.

***

Of flying birds and beasts that craw,
cock and dog are marked out for a fall.
For when within the green gauze screen my love lies sleeping
   On my breast, the cock cries loud and raucous and routs
   Him from his rest. And when he comes to the outer gate,
   The dog makes such a snapping, barking flurry that my
   Love must take his leave, departing in a hurry.
Poultry-peddler
dog-meat-mongers, when next you cry outside my gate, you'll
   get
that cock and dog trussed tightly for the plate.

***

White-haired, but wanton still,
she eyed a bright young spark.
Hair dyed black, she panted to the mountaintop, but as she
   crested the topmost ridge a sudden burst of rain stained
   her white collar black and turned her black hair white again.
Thus the matron's
hopes were raised and shattered in a trice.

***

Girls, buy all the heat you can,
early heat, late heat, heat that's been around a year.
If you will buy, girls, buy all that's in your heart of summer dog
    days' heat, when, on a moonswept sleeping bench, your
    love you meet, encoiled whereon you do whatever it is
    makes innards boil, sweat beads rise, and breath come
    rasping harsh. And buy that heat from long midwinter
    nights, when, in the lower warmer corner, your love and you
    are joined beneath the covers, and hands and feet grow
    fidgety, and throat begins to burn, till you're driven to gulp
    large measures of iced rice water stored in the upper corner.
Heat vendor,
of all your many heats on sale, who could be averse to this loving
    pair?
        Sell them not to others: sell them just to me.

***

The monk that slept here must, after all, have been a man.
How I miss him, now he's gone!
I pillowed my head on his pine winter hat and he pillowed his
    on my festive headpiece. With his long robe I covered
    myself and he covered himself with my skirt. In the night
    I awoke to truth: our love filled hat and headpiece.
    Pondering
all next day, my heart was quite undone.

OR

Emerging as a new genre toward the middle of the fifteenth century was the *kasa*. A typical kasa line, as in sijo, consists of four metric segments. This line is repeated with matched pairings and enumerative development. A poem generally concludes in a line of three, five, four, and three syllables (again as in sijo) in the kasa composed by literati and one of four, four, four, and four in the commoner and women's kasa. The simple metric basis of kasa invites inventiveness in everything from the development of a theme, narrative techniques, sequences of imagery, and the speaker's ethos to views of life and the world itself.

Although the kasa resembles the Chinese rhymeprose, or rhapsody (*fu*), in its form and technique, it is neither prose nor rhymed. It is narrative poetry meant to be sung (or chanted in the case of literati kasa). And unlike the three-line sijo, it tells a story, often adhering to a linear temporal and spatial sequence, though frequently without a plot in the sense of a narrative of events with an emphasis on causality.

Kasa are organized by certain patterns; one of the favorites is the succession of seasons. Poems built on the seasonal pattern unfold a series of nature scenes that evoke each phase of the year. This pattern works well, for example, with poems of reclusion, love, exile, and the country house. Another pattern is based on the rhetoric of argument or complaint: the speaker lists the causes of his present state with an enumeration of hardships, as in the poems of exile or unrequited love. Here, too, the seasonal pattern is often used to emphasize aspects of the speaker's tribulation.

Although four extant examples attributed to the monk Naong (Hyegŭn, 1320–1376) are cited as the earliest specimens, they were composed before the invention of the Korean alphabet and recorded long after their composition. Masters of early Chosŏn include Chŏng Ch'ŏl (1537–1594) and Hŏ Nansŏrhŏn (1563–1585). Kasa of late Chosŏn are not only numerous but more varied in subject matter. In addition to poems about the Japanese invasions of 1592–1598 and reclusion, there are poems on exile, pleasure trips, missions undertaken by envoys to China and Japan, cities such as Seoul, the farmer's works and days, and such unconventional subjects as tobacco and the foibles of foolish men and women. From the end of the seventeenth century commoners began to produce kasa of social criticism, love, and lament.

Poems were often composed and transmitted orally—mostly chanted or recited. Authors of the sung kasa are usually unknown. A typical line in the recitation kasa consists of four (sometimes six) metric segments (two to four syllables each), while the sung kasa offers less fluctuation in the number of syllables in each of the four segments. Kasa on social criticism expose social ills—especially the heavy imposition of unjust taxes that force farmers to abandon their land. Some enumerate the disreputable behavior of selfish men and challenge the established Confucian norms of conduct; others castigate the misdeeds of a wife, or of women who prefer the pleasures of the flesh to chastity, or of one who is anxious to find a husband. Others mock Buddhist monks and nuns who break their vows. The kasa written by commoners resist the dominant ideology of the literati and, with humor and satire, challenge their value system. Writers of popular kasa expanded the matter and manner of the genre with realistic and concrete detail, making use especially of onomatopoeic and mimetic words and everyday speech and adapting folk song meters.

MASTER NAONG (1320–1376)[1]

Song of the Pure Land[2]

I, too, am not an exception but a person born into this world.
Upon pondering the impermanence of life, everything seems so
  illusory.
After death I can do nothing about the distressed face of my
  parents.

1. Hyegŭn (1320–1376) was his dharma name; Naong and Kangwŏrhŏn were his cognomens; his secular surname was A. At the age of twenty-one he received the tonsure from Yoyŏn, a Sŏn master at Myojŏk Hermitage. After attaining enlightenment at Hoeam Monastery of Yangju in 1347, he went to Fa-yüan Monastery in Yüan China. Naong received the dharma transmission there from P'ing-shan Ch'u-lin of Lin-chi lineage. He returned to Koryŏ in 1358 and introduced *kanhwa* Sŏn (meditation of observing the critical phrase). He advocated kanhwa Sŏn and the balanced practice of samadhi (concentration) and wisdom. He started *yŏmbul* Sŏn, which combined Sŏn with the invocation of the Buddha's name. Together with T'aego Pou (1301–1381) and Paegun Kyŏnghan (1299–1375), he was regarded as one of the three prominent monks of the later Koryŏ period. His epitaph (written by Yi Saek) and stupa are at Sillŭk Monastery in Yŏju. He had about two thousand disciples of whom Chach'o and Chich'ŏn were outstanding figures. There is one volume of his lectures: *Record of the Dharma Talks of Naong*.

2. Presumed to have been composed by Naong in the late Koryŏ period. Provided the authorship is confirmed, it could well be the first kasa poem. It was orally transmitted among Buddhist devotees, and the first written form did not appear until the early eighteenth century. Six extant versions offer little difference in content. The oldest is included in the second woodblock edition of "Condensed Essentials of Repentance to the Buddha Amitābha, Encouraging Recalling the Buddha" (*Taeamit'a ch'am yakch'oyoram pogwŏn yŏmbulmun*, 1741). This kasa exhorts people to practice calling the Buddha Amitābha's name (that is, mental reflection on the qualities of the Buddha needed to be born in "the Land of Bliss" (Sukhāvatī), a paradise in the western part of the universe. The Buddha Amitābha, who presides over this paradise, vowed to save those who recalled him by having them gain rebirth in his Pure Land.

> Giving this only momentary thought, I will cast away worldly
>   affairs,
> Bid my parents farewell, and enter a numinous mountain,
> With a goosefoot staff, only a gourd cup, and a black robe.[3]
> Through an audience with a spiritual mentor, I will illuminate
>   my mind.
> I will study a thousand scriptures and myriad treatises to catch
>   the six thieves.[4]
> As I enter the mountain of five aggregates[5] astride the horse of
>   emptiness[6]
> With *mo-yeh* sword[7] in hand, mountains[8] are fold upon fold,
> And the mountain of the four signs[9] is very high.
> Cutting away the afflictions caused by the traceless thieves
> Passing in and out of the six sensory gates,[10]
> I will cross over the ocean of the triple world[11]
> In a ship of wisdom.
> As I load it with sentient beings who invoke the Buddha's name,
> And hoist a sail of the one vehicle[12]
> On a mast of the three vehicles,[13]
> The spring wind blows gently,
> And white clouds circle around.

3. The monk's robe.

4. The defilements caused by means of the six sense organs: eye, ear, nose, tongue, body, and mind. Because these defilements could rob people of their meritorious virtue, they were compared to thieves.

5. The fundamental constituents of a living being: form, feeling, perception, volitional actions, and consciousness. The mountain of the five aggregates, therefore, refers to a person.

6. The minds of people.

7. The names of a renowned ancient Chinese sword. In Buddhism it refers to inborn wisdom or a master's wisdom used for the discipline of his students. See *Pi-yen-lu* 9, case 81, *Hsü tsang-ching* 117:204a.

8. Afflictions in people's minds.

9. Grasping at the concepts of self, being, soul, person.

10. The six sense organs were compared to the six gates through which the mind of defilements is believed to pass.

11. The three levels of a world system: desire, subtle form, formless.

12. *Ekayāna*: the one Buddha Vehicle.

13. *Triyāna*: the three paths of the *śrāvaka*, *pratyekabuddha*, and bodhisattva, which Mahayana teachings claim to be expedient teachings, while regarding the one Buddha Vehicle as the only perfect way to the shores of nirvana.

Thinking of humans, I feel sad and dejected.
You who do not call the Buddha's name, how many more lives do
   you intend to live,
So attached to worldly affairs, and give yourself to love and lust?
Twelve hours a day, thirty days in a month,
By when will you attain the peaceful state?[14]
Everyone has the pure Buddha nature.
When will you realize that?
Meritorious virtues numerous as the sands of the Ganges
Are inherently complete, when will you make use of them?
The Pure Land grows distant, and the hells grow closer.
Look, all of you! Plant wholesome roots.[15]
The merits you accrue in this life
You will receive in the next life.
Your greed for a hundred years will in one morning turn to a
   mote of dust.
Invoking the Buddha's name for three days is a treasure that
   could last aeons.
Oh, this treasure will not experience affliction for a thousand
   aeons
And preserve this eternal present for myriad aeons.
Heaven and earth are vast, but can they surpass this mind?
The sun and moon are bright, but can they surpass this mind?
All Buddhas of the three time periods[16] know this mind.
The sentient beings in the six courses[17] forget this mind.
Then when will they stop the transmigration of the triple world?
Giving this only momentary thought, I am awakened to this
   mind.
As I think of Fu Hsi,[18] mountains fold upon fold,
Water flowing flowing, a breeze rustles, flowers are bright,
And pines and bamboos are tall and green.

14. The ultimate state of enlightenment.

15. *Kuśala-mūla*: good qualities, good seed sown by a good life to be reaped later.

16. Past, present, future.

17. The six *gati*, or conditions of sentient existence: hell, the world of hungry ghosts, animals, demons (*asuras*), human beings, and gods.

18. Fu Hsi is said to have been the first to teach the breeding of fish and cattle.

I enter the Land of Highest Joy by crossing the ocean of Flower
    Garland.[19]
The Pure Land is surrounded by the seven-jewel nets,
And the ground is covered with brocade and the seven jewels.[20]
How joyous to behold them!
At the nine-rank lotus tiers[21] flows the invocation of the Buddha's
    name.
Blue cranes, white cranes, parrots, peacocks, golden and blue
    phoenix—
They all invoke the Buddha's name.
As the cool breeze blows, so the invocation grows strong.
How sad!
We humans, what else can we do but call the Buddha's name?
Homage to the Buddha Amitābha.[22]

PP

19. The ocean of Hwaŏm refers to the human world.
20. Gold, silver, lapis lazuli, crystal, agate, ruby, and carnelian.
21. Arrayed in high, middle, and low sectors of a Pure Land, which are each
then divided into high, middle, and low; *Kuan Wu-liang-shou fo ching*, in *Taishō shin-
shū daizōkyō* 12:344c.
22. Skt. "Namo Amitābha-buddhāya."

CHŎNG KŬGIN (1401–1481)

In Praise of Spring

What do you think of my life,
    you who are buried in red dust,
Do I match the dead
    in the pursuit of elegant pleasures?
Between heaven and earth
    there are many men like me,
But buried among hills and groves,
    do I not know the utmost joy?
In a small thatched hut
    before an emerald stream,
Among the thickets of pine and bamboo,
    I play host to the winds and moon.
Winter left us the other day, and
    a new spring has returned.
Peach and apricot blossoms are
    in full bloom in the evening sun,
Green willows and fragrant grasses
    are green in a fine drizzle.
As if in the marks of a chisel,
    as if in strokes of a brush,
The deft skill of the Fashioner of Things[23]
    is truly brilliant everywhere.

23. The Fashioner of Creatures or Mutations (the old man who fashions creatures) is a shaper and molder of matter—a metaphysical principle responsible for the multiplicity and particularity of the phenomenal world. See Edward H. Shafer, "The Idea of Created Nature in T'ang Literature," *Philosophy East and West* 15 (1965): 153–160.

The birds sing coyly in the wood.
>   drunk with spring air.
Nature and I are one,
>   and the pleasure is the same.
I walk about the brushwood gate
>   or sit in the arbor,
Stroll, hum, and chant.
>   The day in the hills is quiet,
Few know the true flavor of leisure.
>   Come, let's go view hills and waters.
Today walk on the fresh grass,
>   tomorrow bathe in the I River.[24]
Gather ferns in the morning,
>   go fishing in the evening.
Let's strain newly matured wine
>   through a turban of kudzu vine,
And drink, keeping count of our cups
>   with the branches of flowering trees.
Gentle breeze quickly rises
>   over the green waters scattering
Clear fragrance on the cups
>   and petals on our clothes.
Let me know when the jug is empty—
>   I dispatch a boy to a tavern.
A grown-up rambles with a stick, and
>   a boy carries it on his shoulder,
Humming a verse we walk slowly.
>   Sitting alone by the stream,
I wash my cup on the fine sand beach
>   and pour wine and, holding a cup,
I look down the clear stream.
>   The peach blossoms float down
From the Peach Blossom Spring[25] nearby.
>   That hill must mark the place.

24. The abode of Ch'eng I (1033–1108), generally referred to as "the master of the I River."

25. For T'ao Ch'ien's literary and political utopia, see James R. Hightower, *The Poetry of T'ao Ch'ien* (Oxford: Clarendon, 1970), pp. 254–258.

Between the pines in a narrow lane,
    with armful of azaleas,
I quickly climb a hilltop
    and sit among the clouds.
A thousand and myriad villages
    are scattered everywhere.
Mist and glow in the sunlight
    are a brocade spread in front.
Spring color is ample
    over the fields once dark.
Fame and name shun me,
    wealth and rank shun me.
Who else is my friend
    but the clear breeze and bright moon?
With a handful of rice and a gourdful of water,[26]
    nothing distracts me.
Well, what do you say
    to a hundred years of a joyful life?

P L

26. *Analects* 6:11 (Waley, pp. 117–118).

CHŎNG CH'ŎL (1537–1594)

Song of Longing

At the time I was born
    I was born to follow my lord.
Our lives were destined to be joined,
    As even the heavens must have known.
When I was young
    my lord loved me.
There was nothing to compare
    with this heart and love.
All that I longed for in this life
    was to live with him.
Now that I am older,
    for what reason have I been put aside?
A few days ago, serving my lord
    I entered the Moon Palace.[27]
How does it happen since then
    that I have descended to this lower world?
Three years it has been
    since my hair, once combed, became tangled.
I have powders and rouge,
    but for whom would I make myself lovely?
The cares that are knotted in my heart
    pile up, layer upon layer.
It is sighs that build up,
    tears that tumble down.
Life has an end;
    cares are limitless.

27. The Moon Palace is literally Kwanghan Kung (Great Cold Palace).

Indifferent time
    is like the flowing of waters.
The seasons, hot and cold, seem to know
    time and return as they go.
Hearing, seeing,
    there are many things to sense.
Briefly the east wind blows
    and melts away the fallen snow.
Two or three branches have bloomed
    on the plum tree outside the window:
a bold brightness,
    a fragrance deep and mysterious.
At dusk the moon
    shines by the bedside
as if sensing him, rejoicing
    —Is it my lord; could it be?
I wonder, if I broke off that blossom
    and sent it to the place where my lord stays,
what would he think
    as he looked at it?

Blossoms fall, new leaves appear,
    and shade covers.
Silk curtains are lonely;
    embroidered curtains are opened.
I close the lotus screen
    and open the peacock screen . . .
How can a day be so tedious,
    so full of cares?
I spread open the mandarin duck quilt,
    take out the five-colored thread,
measure it with a golden ruler
    and make a cloak for my lord
with skill,
    with taste.

Gazing toward the place where my lord stays
    I think of sending to him
these clothes in a jade white chest

on a pack frame of coral,
but he is so far, so far,
    like a mountain, or a cloud.
Who is there to seek him out
    over the road of ten thousand *ri?*
When it reached him and was opened,
    would he be pleased?

At night a frost falls;
    the wild goose passes over with a cry.
Alone, I climb the tower
    and open the jade curtain.
Above East Mountain the moon has risen
    and far to the north a star appears.
Is it my lord? Happy,
    tears come unbidden.
Let me extract this brightness
    and send it to the Phoenix Tower:
fix it to the tower
    and illuminate all directions,
that even the deepest mountains and valleys
    may be as bright as day.

Heaven and earth are blockaded
    under a white monochrome.
Men, even birds on the wing
    have disappeared.
With the cold so intense
    here, far to the south,[28]
in the lofty Phoenix Tower,
    how much colder it must be!
Would that the sunny spring could be sent
    to warm the place where my lord stays,
or that the sunlight bathing the thatched eaves
    might be sent to the Phoenix Tower.

28. In the original the two rivers Hsiao and Hsiang that flow into Lake Tungt'ing in Hunan, rich in mythology and scenic beauty.

I tuck my red skirt up,
    roll my blue sleeves halfway,
and, as the day declines, by high, thin bamboos
    I lean on a staff, lost in thought.
The brief sun sinks swiftly;
    the long night settles aloft.

I set the inlaid lute
    by the side of the blue lamp
and rest, hoping
    to see my lord, even in a dream.
Cold, cold is the quilt!
    O, when will night become day?

Twelve times each day,
    thirty days each month,
I try, even for a moment, not to think,
    that I may forget these cares,
but they are knotted within my heart,
    they have pierced through my bones.
Even though ten doctors like P'ien Ch'üeh came,[29]
    what could they do with this illness?
Alas, my illness
    is because of my lord.

I would rather die and become
    a swallowtail butterfly.
I would light upon each flowering branch
    one after another, as I went,
till I settled, with perfumed wings
    upon the garments of my lord.
O, my lord, though you forget my existence,
    I shall attend you.

DM

29. A famous physician during the Spring and Autumn period; *Shih chi* 105:2785–2820.

Continued Song of Longing

"Lady, who goes there?
    You look so familiar.
Why did you leave
    the White Jade Capital in the heavens,[30]
whom do you seek
    as the sun goes down?"

"Oh, it's you!
    Hear my story now.
My face and ways
    do not merit my lord's favor.
Yet he deigns to recognize me
    when we meet.
I believed in him
    with undivided heart.
I flirted and displayed my charm—
    I might have annoyed him.
His welcoming face
    has changed from the past.
Reclining, I ponder;
    seated, I calculate:
my sins,
    piled high as the mountains;
I don't quarrel with heaven,
    I don't blame men.
I try to untie this sadness—
    it was the Fashioner's doing."

30. Where the Taoist deities reside.

"Fret not, my dear.
    Something eats at my heart, too.
I've served him;
    I know him.
His face once placid as water
    shows little enough of peace these days.
Spring cold and summer heat,
    how did he spend them?
Autumn days and winter skies,
    who served them?
Morning gruel and daily rice,
    did he have enough?
Do you think he slept well
    these long winter nights?"

"I yearn for word of him,
    how I long to hear his news!
But the day is done.
    Will someone come tomorrow?
Oh, tormenting thought!
    Where shall I go?
Led and pushed
    when I climb a high hill,
clouds gather,
    and—why—a mist, too!
When hills and waters are dark,
    how can I see the sun and moon?
What can I see even an inch away?
    A thousand miles is so far . . .
I'll go down to the sea
    and wait for a boat.
Winds and waves
    in turmoil, in shambles.
The boatman is gone;
    only the empty ship . . .
Standing alone by the river,
    I gaze far into the setting sun.
News from my lord
    is out of the question!

I return when darkness creeps
 under the eaves of my hut.
For whom does that lamp
 burn in the middle of the wall?
Over hill and valley I go,
 back and forth, aimlessly.
Exhausted,
 I sink into sleep.
At last my prayer is answered,
 and I see him in a dream.
But time has stolen
 his face once like jade.
I would tell him all,
 all my heart desires.
But tears flow on and on,
 and I cannot speak.
Unable to tell of my love,
 words stick in my throat.
A frivolous rooster
 wakes me from my slumber.
Ah, everything was a mocking dream.
 Where is my fair one?
Sitting up in my sleep,
 I open the window.
Only the pitiable shadow
 follows me.
I'd sooner die
 and be the setting moon
and shine
 in his window."

"The moon, say you, my lady?
 Rather, a driving rain."[31]

31. The lady of Witches' Mountain appeared in King Hsiang's (298–265 B.C.) dream and said to him: "I live on the southern side of the Witches' Mountain, in the rocky crags of Kao-ch'iu. At dawn I am the Morning Cloud, and at dusk the Driving Rain." See Lois Fusek, "The 'Kao-t'ang Fu,' " *Monumenta Serica* 30 (1972–1973):413.

Little Odes on Mount Star

An unknown guest in passing
    stopped on Mount Star and said:
"Listen, Master of Mist Settling Hall
    and Resting Shadow Arbor,
despite the many pleasures
    life held,
why did you prefer to them all
    this mountain, this water?
What made you choose
    the solitude of hills and streams?"
Sweeping away the pine needles,
    setting a cushion on a bamboo couch,
I casually climb into the seat
    and view the four quarters.
Floating clouds at the sky's edge come and go
    nestling on Auspicious Stone Terrace;[32]
their flying motion and gentle gestures
    resemble our host.
White waves in the blue stream
    rim the arbor;
as if someone stitched and spread
    the cloud brocade of the Weaver Star,
the water rushes
    in endless patterns.
On other mountains without a calendar
    who would know the year's cycle?

32. The summit of Mount Mudŭng in Kwangju.

Here every subtle change of the seasons
    unrolls before us.
Whether you hear or see,
    this is truly the land of tanscendents.
The morning sun at the window with plum trees—
    the fragrance of blossoms wakes me.
Who says there is nothing
    to keep an old hermit busy?
In the sunny spot under the hedges
    I sow melons,
tie the vines, support them;
    when rain nurtures the plants,
I think of the old tale
    of the Blue Gate.[33]
Tying my straw sandals,
    grasping a bamboo staff,
I follow the peach blossom causeway
    over to Fragrant Grass Islet.
As I stroll to the West Brook,
    the stone screen painted by nature
in the bright moonlit mirror
    accompanies me.
Why seek Peach Blossom Spring?[34]
    Earthly paradise is here.
The casual south wind
    scatters green shade;
a faithful cuckoo,
    where did he come from?
I wake from dozing
    on the pillow of ancient worthies[35]
and see the hanging wet balcony
    floating on the water.

33. The southeast gate of Ch'ang-an. When the dynasty changed, Shao P'ing, marquis of Tung-ling under the Ch'in, had to live by raising melons. His melons were called Blue Gate or Tung-ling melons. See Watson, *Records* 1:130.

34. See Highwater, *The Poetry of T'ao Ch'ien*, pp. 254–258.

35. The ancient worthy refers to a hermit said to have lived before the time of Fu Hsi, a Chinese culture hero.

With my kudzu cap aslant
  and my hemp smock tucked into my belt,
I go nearer
  to watch the frolicking fishes.
After the rain overnight,
  here and there, red and white lotus;
their fragrance rises into the still sky
  filling myriad hills.
As though I had met with Chou Tun-i[36]
  and questioned him on the Ultimate Secret—
as though an immortal Great Unique[37]
  had shown me the Jade Letters—
I look across Cormorant Rock
  by Purple Forbidden Shallows;
a tall pine tree screens the sun,
  I sit on the stone path.
In the world of man it is the sixth month;
  here it is autumn.
A duck bobbing on the limpid stream
  moves to a white sandbar,
makes friends with the gulls,
  and dozes away.
Free and at leisure,
  it resembles our host.
At the fourth watch the frost moon rises
  over the phoenix trees.
Thousand cliffs, ten thousand ravines,
  could they be brighter by daylight?
Who moved the Crystal Palace
  from Huchou?[38]
Did I jump over the Milky Way
  and climb into the Moon Palace?

36. Chou (1017–1073) is the author of *The Diagram of the Supreme Ultimate Explained*, which elucidates the origins of "Heavenly Principles."

37. T'ai-i (Great One or Unique One), the supreme sky god in Chinese mythology who resides in the palace at the Center of Heaven, marked by the polestar. See Needham, *Science and Civilization in China* 3:260.

38. On Mount West Lake in Hu-chou.

Leaving behind a pair of old pines
    on the fishing terrace,
I let my boat drift downstream
    as it pleases,
passing pink knotweeds
    and a sandbar of white cloverfern.
When did we reach
    the Dragon Pool below Jade Ring Hall?
Moved by a sunset glow,
    cowherds
in green pastures by the crystal river
    blow on their pipes.
They might awaken the dragon
    sunk deep at the pool's bottom.
Emerging from mists and ripples,
    cranes might abandon their nests
and soar into midair.
    Su Shih in his poem on Red Cliff
praises the seventh month;[39]
    but why do people cherish
the mid-autumn moon?
    When thin clouds part,
and waves grow still,
    the rising moon
anchors herself in a pine branch.
    How extravagant! Li Po drowned
trying to scoop up the reflected moon.
    North winds sweep away
the heaped leaves on empty hills,
    marshal the clouds,
drive the snow.
    The Creator loves to fashion—
he makes snowflowers of white jade,
    devises thousands of trees and forests.

39. "In the autumn of the year *jen-hsü*, the seventh month, when the moon had just passed its prime, a friend and I went out in a small boat to amuse ourselves at the foot of the Red Cliff"; see Watson, *Su Tung-p'o*, p. 87.

The shallows in front freeze over.
　　A monk crosses over
the one-log bridge aslant,
　　a staff on his shoulder.
What temple are you headed for?
　　Don't boast of
the recluse's riches
　　lest some find out
this lustrous, hidden world.
　　Alone, deep in the mountains,
with the classics, pile on pile,
　　I think of the men
of all times:
　　many were sages,
many were heroes.
　　Heavenly intent goes
into the making of men.
　　Yet fortunes
rise and fall;
　　chance seems unknowable,
and sadness deep.
　　Why did Hsü Yu on Mount Chi
cleanse his innocent ears?[40]
　　When he threw away his last gourd,
his integrity became even nobler.
　　Man's mind is like his face—
new each time one sees it.
　　Worldly affairs are like clouds—
how perilous they are!
　　The wine made yesterday
must be ready:
　　passing the cup back and forth,
let's pour more wine till we're tired.
　　Then our hearts will open,
the net of sorrow unravel to nothing.

40. When Emperor Yao wished to make the recluse Hsü Yu his successor, the latter went into hiding. At the emperor's second offer, Hsü Yu went to the Ying River to cleanse his ears.

String the black zither
and pluck "Wind in the Pines."[41]
    We have all forgotten
Who is host and who is guest.
    The crane flying through the vast sky
is the true immortal in this valley—
    I must have met him
on the Jasper Terrace under the moon.
    The guest addresses the host with a word:
"You, sir, you alone are immortal."

41. The name of a *tz'u* (lyric) tune.

PAK ILLO (1561–1643)

Song of Peace

Long and narrow, our land remained secluded
    to the east of the Yellow Sea.
Through the ages we followed
    the pure and honest ways of Chi Tzu.[42]
For two centuries since the dynasty's founding,
    we upheld the rites and justice,
and our civilization matched
    the glory of Han, T'ang, and Sung.
But one morning
    a million island savages
clashed with millions of innocent souls,
    resolved to follow the glint of the sword.
Bones lay in heaps
    on the plain,
majestic cities and imposing towns
    became lairs for wolves and foxes.
Cold and lonely,
    the royal carriage sped north
in the smoke and dust
    that gauzed the sunlight.
The Ming emperor, marvelous and valiant,
    cast a deadly roar
and cut down with a single sword
    the wicked Japanese raiders at P'yŏngyang.

42. The uncle of the last monarch of the Shang, who is said to have fled to
Korea in 1122 B.C. when the Shang were deposed by the Chou and to have built a
capital at P'yŏngyang. Traditionally his dynasty lasted until 194 B.C.

Like the wind, he spurred his troops southward,
　　pressing the enemy hard to the shore.
We did not storm the cornered pirates,[43]
　　but besieged them for several years.
And to the east of the Naktong River
　　the pick of our army, like lofty clouds,
met a great tactician and general,[44]
　　and, under his five brilliant virtues,[45]
our soldiers became hunters of wild dogs.
　　The humanity and bravery of our heroes
blended with the eloquence of a mediator.[46]
　　Peace settled again in the south,
and soldiers and horses gathered strength, waiting.
　　But one evening
a storm broke again,
　　and generals like dragons,
soldiers like clouds,
　　under the royal standard that covered the sky[47]
spread out along frontiers myriad miles long.
　　Hills shook
with the battle cry;
　　generals led the van
and rushed the enemy
　　like thunderbolts in a tempest.
Callow Captain Kiyomasa[48]
　　was in our grasp;
but tired soldiers,
　　in the trying rain,

43. *Sun Tzu* 7:28b–34a; see Samuel B. Griffith, *Sun Tzu: The Art of War* (Oxford: Clarendon, 1963). p. 110: "Do not press an enemy at bay."

44. Refers to Sŏng Yunmun (fl. 1591–1607), Regional Commander of the Left Bank. The original text compares him to Chu-ko Liang (181–234), reputed to be the greatest Chinese strategist of all time.

45. Wisdom, sincerity, benevolence, courage, and strictness.

46. Refers to the Ming mediator between Korea and Japan, Shen Wei-ching. On eloquence see *Book of Songs* 260:3 (Karlgren, *Book of Odes*, pp. 228–229).

47. Su Shih, "The Red Cliff, I" (Watson, *Su T'ung-p'o*, p. 98): "The stems and sterns of his [Ts'ao Ts'ao; 155–220] ships touched for a thousand miles, and his flags and pennants blocked out the sky."

48. A pejorative reference to Katō Kiyomasa (1562–1611).

raised the siege,
> stiffened morale.
The raiders then ran in the four directions;
> we may not catch them all alive.
Their caves,
> once so strong,
are now heaps of ashes—
> a natural fastness is not all in a battle.[49]
Since the lofty virtue of the Son of Heaven
> and the abundant favors of our king
extend far and near,
> heaven punished the wily bandits with death
and manifested humanity and justice.
> Was it yesterday that we sang of peace?[50]
Even the idle
> became his majesty's men,
fought desperately to repay his favor,
> fought east and west for seven years
to lay down their lives for their country.
> Today, once again, peace reigns over the land,
and we return to the willowed barracks[51]
> putting our spears aside.
Songs of peace
> and drums and horns
are loud as the laughter of dragons and fishes
> that reside deep in the Palace of the Dragon King.

49. Mencius 2B:1 (Lau, *Mencius*, p. 85): "Heaven's favorable weather is less important than Earth's advantageous terrain, and Earth's advantageous terrain is less important than human unity."

50. *Han-shih wai-chuan* 5:12; J. R. Hightower, *Han Shih Wai Chuan: Han Ying's Illustrations of the Didactic Application of the Classic of Songs* (Cambridge: Harvard University Press, 1952), pp. 171–172: "In the time of great peace there are no sudden winds or violent rains or waves and inundations on the sea."

51. Hsi-liu Ying in the southwest of Hsien-yang in Shensi, where troops under Chou Ya-fu (d. 143 B.C.) once made their encampment. See H. H. Dubs, *The History of the Former Han Dynasty* (Baltimore: Waverly Press, 1938) 1:269–299, 326, and n. 8.6: "In B.C. 174 he was appointed to a command against the Hsiung-nu, who were then invading the empire, and when the Emperor Wen presented himself at his stronghold, his Majesty was unable to gain admittance until Chou himself had given orders for the gate to be opened."

Royal banners, too, in the west wind
    flutter aslant,
like five-hued lucky clouds
    hanging in the sky.
A scene of peace
    spreads endless and happy.
Raising the bow, lifting the arrow,
    we sing the triumphal chant
as if to outdo one another.
    Our joyous song gathers in the emerald sky.
Overcome with joy,
    with three-foot sword, keen and bright,
I lift my face and whistle a tune;
    when I stand up ready to dance,
the magic sword that I lifted high
    shines between the Plow and the Weaver.
Hands dance, feet leap,
    naturally,
as we praise and dance the seven martial virtues[52]
    never wishing to stop.
Of all the joyous things in life,
    is there anything like this?
Where is Mount Hua?[53]
    I'll dispatch the news.
Where are Heaven Mountains?[54]
    I'll suspend an arrow on it.

52. While T'ang T'ai-tsung, still as the Prince of Ch'in, was subjugating the four quarters, there was a piece of music named "Ch'in-wang p'o-chen-yüeh" in circulation. The earliest record of its performance dates from 627. In 633 T'ai-tsung ordered the choreographic diagram "P'o-chen-wu t'u" to be drawn up and instructed Lü Ts'ai to teach one hundred and twenty musicians to perform the dance according to the diagram. Later this dance was called the Dance of the Seven Virtues. The first reference to the seven virtues occurs in the *Tso Commentary*, Duke Hsüan 12 (Legge 5:320). They are as follows: repressing cruelty, calling in the weapons of war, preserving the great appointment, firmly establishing one's merit, giving repose to the people, harmonizing all the state, and enlarging the general wealth.

53. Mount Hua is the western sacred mountain in Kiangsu.

54. In Hsin-chiang.

Now let's be
    loyal and filial.
Idle,
    I lie asleep in the camp
and ask
    in what dynasty I live.
The golden days of Fu Hsi,[55] of course.
    As heaven does not send down a long rain,
the sun grows brighter.
    The bright white sun
shines upon the world.
    Old men scattered
in ditches and moats[56]
    return home[57]
like swallows on the spring breeze.
    Who would not feel happy
when they can't forget their hometown!
    Tell me of the joy
of your return;
    Oh, unscathed people,[58]
think of the royal favor that saved you.
    Under his profound grace,
brighten the five norms,
    nurture the people to build up the nation's power—
they would then rise and march on their own.
    Heaven, we know,
returned luck to favor us.

55. A Chinese culture hero, inventor of writing, fishing, and trapping.

56. *Mencius* 2B:4 (Lau, p. 88): "In the years of the famine close on a thousand of your people suffered, the old and the young being abandoned in the gutter, the able-bodied scattered in all directions."

57. James Legge, *The Li Ki* (Oxford: Clarendon, 1885), p. 131: "The ancients had a saying, that a fox, when dying, adjusts its head in the direction of the mound [where it was whelped]; manifesting thereby [how it shares in the feeling of] humility."

58. *Book of Songs* 258:3 (Karlgren, *Book of Odes*, pp. 223 f.): "The drought is excessive, it cannot be removed; it is fearsome, it is terrible, like lightning, like thunder; of the crowd of people that remained of the Chou, there is not an undamaged body left."

So we pray that you bless our dynasty,
that the royal house be endless,
that the sun and moon of the Three Dynasties[59]
shine on the golden age of Yao and Shun,
that there be no more war
for myriad years,
that people till the fields and dig wells
and sing the praises of peace,[60]
that we always have a holy king above us,
and that he and we share the joy of peace.

59. The dynasties of Hsia, Shang (Yin), and Chou.

60. A song that eulogized the blessing of peace under Emperor Yao (*Ku-shih yüan* [*SPPY*] 1:1a); translated by Watson in *The Columbia Book of Chinese Poetry* (1984), p. 70.

Lament on the Water

My king summoned this sick and aged body
    and dispatched me as a shipmaster.
Thus do I travel down to Pusan
    in the sultry summer month of the *ŭlsa* year.[61]
Sick as I am, I dare not sit still
    in this gateway, the strategic portal.
Wearing a long sword aslant
    boldly I step aboard the warship,
muster my courage,
    and stare with scorn at Tsushima.
The yellow clouds that chase the winds
    are gathered up here, gathered up there,
and the dim green waves
    and the endless sky are one.
I wander about on the ship
    recalling the past;
my foolish mind
    reproaches the Yellow Emperor.[62]
Since the boundless sea
    surrounds heaven and earth,
what barbarians will cross
    myriad miles of winds and waves
and dare to encroach upon our shores?

61. The year 1605.
62. The Yellow Emperor was thought to be the inventor of wheeled vehicles, ships, armor, and pottery, among other things.

Why on earth did people
learn to build ships?
Throughout the ages,
everywhere under heaven,[63]
they have become an endless evil,
fostering sorrow in the people's heart.
Ah, I realize now
it is the First Emperor's fault.
Granted that ships had to be made,
if the Japanese were not bred there,
would empty ships have started out
for Tsushima by themselves?
The First Emperor believed in empty words
and sent maidens and boys to solitary isles[64]
to procure the pills of immortality.
Thus he spawned unruly bandits
on those islands[65]
and brought great indignation and shame
upon the Middle Kingdom.
How many immortality pills
did he obtain,
and did they bring him a life
long as the Great Wall he built?
He, too, was a mortal,
I cannot see what he gained.
When I consider the matter carefully,
Hsü Shih[66] and his like went too far.
Could he seek refuge elsewhere
as a loyal subject?
He did not see the spirits;
but had he returned,

63. *Book of Songs* 205:2 (Waley, p. 320).

64. *Shih chi* 6:247.

65. Here the poet argues that descendents of those "boys and maidens" settled on Japanese islands and became the ancestors of the Japanese people.

66. Or Hsü Fu, who persuaded the First Emperor of Ch'in to send out an expedition of several thousand young men and women to search for the Isles of the Blest, thought to be inhabited by immortals. See, for example, Po Chü-i's poem "Magic" in Arthur Waley, *A Hundred and Seventy Chinese Poems* (New York: Knopf, 1919), pp. 195–196.

our naval men
>   would not have lamented at all.
Forget them all!
>   No use blaming the past.
Let's stop this idle dispute
>   between right and wrong.
Calmly, I meditate:
>   I was too obstinate.
The shipbuilding of the Yellow Emperor
>   was not so bad after all.
Had there been no ships,
>   how could Chang Han[67] rouse his spirits
when the autumn breeze caresses him,
>   how could he return south of the river,
when the sky is clear and the sea broad?
>   How can a fisherman travel
without a boat
>   to enjoy his life free as duckweed,
a life better than that of three dukes,[68]
>   among matchless hills and waters?
Judging from these,
>   a system of ships
seems worthy of praise.
>   And why should we not be elated
sitting astride a darting boat
>   day and night
as we sing of the moon fronting the winds?
>   In olden days
wine tables crowded ships;[69]
>   today,

67. Chang (c. 258–319) took office with Prince Ching of Ch'i but resigned because "he could not do without the salad and bream of the Sung River in Kiangsu"; *Chin shu* (Peking: Chunghua, 1974) 92:2384.

68. This phrase comes from a poem by Tai Shih-ping, "Shih-ping shih-chi" (*SPTK hsü-pien* 1) 7:5b. The three dukes were originally the three ministers of state in Chou—the grand tutor, the grand assistant, and the grand guardian—but in Korea the term *three dukes* refers to the chief, second, and third state counselors.

69. Su Shih, "The Red Cliff, 1" (Watson, *Su Tung-p'o*, p. 90): "Among the litter of cups and bowls, we lay down in a heap in the bottom of the boat, unaware that the east was already growing light."

only large swords and long spears.
  A ship it is,
but not as ships once were.
  Therefore sorrow and joy,
too, differ.
  From time to time
I gaze at the polestar;[70]
  the tears of an old man
deplore the age.
  Our civilization
is bright as Han, T'ang, and Sung.
  But fortune deserted our dynasty,
and the crafty designs of pirates
  made us harbor lasting regrets.
We've not yet wiped out this shame,
  not even one hundredth.
However incapable,
  I am your subject.
The way of success being different today,
  I have grown old without serving at your side.
But my anxious heart
  is always with you.
Firmness of will and apprehension for my country
  grow stronger as I grow old.
Insignificant and ill
  as I am,
when can I cleanse this shame
  and redress this grief ?
The dead Chu-ko Liang
  chased the living Ssu-ma I,[71]

70. *Analects* 2:1; see Arthur Waley, *The Analects of Confucius* (London: Allen and Unwin, 1949), p. 88: "The Master said, He who rules by moral force (*te*) is like the polestar, which remains in its place while all the lesser stars do homage to it."

71. An allusion to the story of Ssu-ma I (178–251), who was frightened by the dead Chu-ko Liang (181–234): "In this month [Chu-ko] Liang died, with the army. The *chiang-shih* Yang I put the army in order and marched off; the population rushed off to Ssu-ma I and informed him, and I pursued them. Chiang Wei ordered [Yang] I to turn the banners and beat the drums, as if intending to meet I. I thereupon departed with his troops in battle formation. Entering [Yeh-] ku he

and the limbless Sun Pin
    captured P'ang Chüan.[72]
How then should I—
    Still alive, four limbs intact—
should I fear
    thieves of mice and dogs?
When I charge the enemy ships,
    descend upon them,
they'll be fallen leaves
    in frosty winds.
By freeing them and seizing them seven times[73]
    we too will succeed like Chu-ko Liang.
O wriggling island savages,
    beg quickly for surrender!
You know those who yield are set free—
    so yield now and avoid disaster.
The eminent virtues of our king
    dictate that all men live together.
In a peaceful world,
    we live under another sage ruler,
with his virtues
    bright as the sun and moon.
And we who have ridden on battle ships
    will soon sing in a fishing boat
in autumn moon and spring breeze,
    and laying our heads on high pillows,
we'll see once more the happy era
    when all the waters sing in unison.[74]

                                           PL

---

announced the death of [Chu-ko Liang]. The people made it a saying, "Dead Chu-ko has put live Chung-ta to flight!" See Achilles Fang, *The Chronicles of the Three Kingdoms* (Cambridge: Harvard University Press, 1952), pp. 435–436.

72. An allusion to the story of how Sun Pin of Ch'i defeated the Wei army of P'ang Chüan (*Shih chi* 65:2162).

73. An allusion to the story of Chu-ko Liang, the chief minister of Liu Pei of the Shu kingdom, capturing and releasing Meng Hao seven times. See *San-kuo chih* 35, *Shu shu* 5:911–937, especially. p. 921.

74. See note 50 above.

ANONYMOUS

Song of a Foolish Wife

I do not mean to speak harshly of her,
    but look at what that woman does:
Married for only three months,
    she already laments that her life is harsh.
She writes a letter to her parents,
    speaking ill of her new in-laws:
"How covetous is my father-in-law!
    how jealous is my mother-in law!
That sister-in-law has a big mouth,
    my older brother-in-law's wife is so severe!
Look at my younger brother-in-law's wicked wife,
    and my husband's bitchy concubine, scheming like a fox;
Those wild and willful male and female slaves,
    going in and out, doing nothing but slandering;
Even though I still trusted my dear husband,
    he fell to their side like a tree chopped ten times."
From here to there, she does nothing but complain,
    from this corner to that, she makes only false accusations.
Saying she cannot live with her in-laws,
    pouring poisonous water from the bottle to feign suicide,
Running away with her skirt pulled over her face,
    she flees from home, packing a bundle,
    coming or going, unable to bear her marriage:
"Shall I follow a group of wandering monks,
    with a long bamboo stick as my friend?
Should I go sightseeing in the field?"
    She idles away her time having her fortune told.
Outwardly seeming full of troubles,
    inwardly full of secret plans,

Putting on light powder, drawing eyebrows as her job,
    she spends her days plucking out hair.
When admonished by her mother-in-law,
    she cannot be outdone by even a single word.
When her husband becomes anxious,
    she is certain to retort defiantly:
Impulsively she fancies that lamp-lighting man,
    should I change my lot with him?
She does nothing but brag about her noble lineage:
    "Should I open a shady tavern?"
That Ppaengttŏk's mother outside the South Gate,
    her nature—was she born like that?
Her nature was perhaps learned,
    as she grew up with no one to follow after,
Confronting two parties with each other,
    she spends her time interrogating and defending.
Spreading gossip from here to there,
    she returns home to complain about the food;
No thought to worshiping her ancestors,
    her only deed is to offer a Buddhist ceremony;
She even gives out all her clothes
    to the noisy ritual by shamans and blind ones.
When you look at her husband's frame,
    he is like the hind leg of a shaggy dog;
When you look at the doings of her son,
    he is like a feather-plucked kite.
Taffy peddlers, rice-cake peddlers,
    she calls them all in, her children as an excuse.
In front of a spinning wheel, she lets out a yawn,
    in front of a cotton gin, she takes a stretch.
Alienating one family from another,
    telling obscene and indecent tales is her job;
She makes the guiltless eat shit through slander,
    her furnishings dwindle away,
    her worries increase more and more.
Her skirt becomes shorter and shorter,
    her waist becomes longer and longer.
In her worn-out straw shoes without the outer rim,
    carrying her young child on her back,
At every house holding marriages or funerals,

getting free food is her job;
At children's fights and grown-ups' fights,
    she makes the blameless suffer floggings;
She becomes angry without reason,
    and beats her dear child;
Since she drove out her daughter-in-law,
    her son is now a widower.
Since she dragged her daughter back home,
    she brings ruin to her daughter's new family.
How odd that she claps her two hands,
    wailing out loudly!
Finding fault for an unknown reason,
    she lays down her head, wrapped around with a cloth as if ill;
Since she runs away with an illicit lover,
    how many times was she enslaved by the king's men?
Oh, you ignorant living beings,
    look closely at what she does.
If you've heard good advice,
    make it your job to practice it.

Song of an Old Maid

You there!
    Listen, please, to my sorrowful words.
Since humans and myriad things came into being,
    animals and birds, grass and trees, all have their mates.
A man created in the world
    possesses honor, riches, and offspring.
My pitiful lot is so perilous and harsh,
    is there another like me?
Even though you live all of a hundred years,
    there are only thirty-six thousand days.
If I live alone, do I live for a thousand years?
    If I remain a virgin,
    do I live for ten thousand?
My unresourceful parents,
    being poor and belonging to petty nobility,
act like high nobility, keeping proper duties,
    their posturing still bungled,
Devoted to outrageous words and deeds
    while their single daughter is getting old.
In a desolate, empty room,
    I sit alone, deserted,
Tossing and turning, I cannot sleep.
    Listen, please, to my solitary complaints.
My senile mother and father,
    why did you raise me?
Bringing me up until I die,
    will they butcher me, or bake me for food?
From men and women created during Emperor of Mankind,

traces made during Fu Hsi,
Human beings choosing mates and marrying,
    it has been so since the old days.
I know a maiden with lot so fortunate,
    she is married before twenty.
Descendents of people, marrying a man, marrying a woman,
    even though these are all respectable deeds,
My pitiful lot is so sinister,
    I am a maid even until forty.
If I knew I would be thus,
    I should not have come out from the beginning,
A moonlit gauze window, during long, long nights,
    unable to sleep full of worries
In my desolate, empty room,
    pacing hither and thither,
Thinking of my future days,
    my heart grows heavier and heavier.
My only father is half-witted,
    my only mother cannot tell beans from barley;
When the day breaks, it is tomorrow,
    when the year ends, it is next year.
Neglecting marriage complaints,
    my parents only complain of poverty.
When a guest arrives from somewhere,
    could he perchance be a matchmaker?
I inquire after a child demanding an answer,
    only the officer demanding to fulfill the village compact
    and duty of returning the loaned grain;
Oh, a letter from somewhere,
    could it be a marriage proposal?
I ask the child again,
    it is a funeral notice of my maternal uncle.
Oh, how tragic and agonizing!
    What shall I do about my aching heart?
That child in the house in front
    is already having a child.
That surly woman in the house out back
    is getting married today or tomorrow.
That heartless time of past days,

I would unknot it after getting married,
But my parents are heartless,
    do not think of me.
Do not consider riches and honors,
    if his looks and bearings seem suitable.
Is a forty-year-old maiden young?
    Please prepare my marriage things.
Kim Tongi is a widower,
    Yi Tongi threw out his wife.
Granny matchmaker is nowhere to be seen,
    why is there no one asking for me?
The black cow is now well fattened,
    we also have rice and dry paddies for ancestral rites;
You look for a scholar official of good family,
    making me get so old like this?
I have lipstick and powder,
    but put them away;
Black skirt and white blouse,
    I placed them in front of a lighted mirror;
My dark eyebrows like the Moon Mountain,
    my slender waist like a fine willow;
Oh, how beautiful is my countenance,
    oh, how exquisite my demeanor!
In this time flowing endlessly,
    oh, how pitiful is my demeanor!
I speak to the mirror:
    Oh, how oppressive my fate!
Nowhere to go, not even me,
    no use for you, not even you.
My father the Minister of War,
    my grandfather the Minister of Finance;
Since my lineage is like this,
    how difficult to follow the custom.[75]
It is already spring,
    grass, trees, and all living things take delight,
Azaleas in full blossom everywhere,
    grass sends out new shoots;

75. That is, she can marry a member of the ruling elite, not a commoner.

Decayed and wilted bamboo fences rustle and crinkle,
    a lark flies up high in the sky.
Spring breeze, night moon, and fine rain,
    how can I sleep alone in an empty room?
You devilish children,
    do not speak such words:
A groom comes to the house in front,
    a bride leaves the house in the back.
Things I have heard with my ears,
    so many things I have felt.
The sun sets over green willows and beautiful grass,
    why do the years go by so easily?
Our lives are like morning dew,
    unexpectedly getting old.
With my flowing lock on my side,
    All I can do is sigh.
No mate for my long nights,
    no friend for my long days.
Sitting and lying down,
    I think these thoughts again and again,
Perhaps my wretched life itself
    is my enemy, since I cannot die!

C S

Chinese logographs and classics were introduced into ancient Korean kingdoms as early as the second century B.C. In Koguryŏ, a Chinese-style royal academy was established in the late fourth century, and the learned class studied the Five Classics, histories, and the *Selections of Refined Literature* (*Wen hsüan*), compiled by Hsiao T'ung (501–531). Paekche had scholars of the Five Classics as well, and it was they who transmitted Chinese primers and Confucian canonical texts to Japan. In Silla, monuments erected at the sites of King Chinhŭng's tours of inspection, all from the mid-sixth century, show the mastery of written Chinese. Proficiency in Chinese enabled the compilation of national histories in Paekche around 375, in Silla in 545, and in Koguryŏ in 600. Thus Chinese was used in state archives, diplomatic papers, and inscriptions, as well as to teach Confucian texts and Buddhist scriptures.

In 640 sons of the royal family were sent to China to study Confucian texts. Later 216 students traveled to T'ang China to spend a term of ten years there and pass the civil service examination for foreigners. By 907, 58 Silla nationals had passed the T'ang examination. The most famous among them was Ch'oe Ch'iwŏn, who at age twelve went to China where he passed the examination at the age of eighteen (874). Upon his return to Korea, lamenting his country's social disorder, Ch'oe retired to Mount Kaya and is said to have become a transcendent. He was posthumously enfeoffed as Marquis of Bright Culture in 1023.

With the establishment of the royal academy in Silla in 682, the core curriculum consisted of the *Analects* and the *Book of Filial Piety*, along with specialization in the *Book of Songs*, the *Book of Changes*, the *Book of Documents*, the *Record of Rites*, the *Tso Commentary*, or *Selections of Refined Literature*. In Koryŏ the examination system was instituted in 958 to recruit civil officials and staff the bureaucracy; by 992 the royal academy was established in the capital. With the examination system in place, old-style poetry and parallel prose gradually gave way to new-style poetry and old-style prose—the prose of the Han and poetry of the T'ang and Sung began to be studied and imitated.

Scholar-officials continued to occupy the dominant position in Chosŏn they had held in Koryŏ. Courtier poets wrote on every conceivable social occasion; they must have dreamed in verse as well, for numerous poems were inspired by dreams. They wrote poems on the walls of monasteries, post stations, or friends' houses, if the host happened to be out. Such impromptu poems were mulled over, harmonized, and treasured. In addition to poems on nature, friendship and wine, and time, they wrote on moral cultivation, social problems, and yearning for freedom from political reality. Because poetry occupied the highest place in the literary hierarchy, and most of their energy was spent in producing poems, some were quite prolific—Yi Kyubo wrote more than two thousand poems, for example, Yi Saek and Sŏ Kŏjŏng about six thousand. If a soldier, merchant, slave, or female entertainer is mentioned in history, it is because of that person's ability to write poetry in literary Chinese. This ability also saved the lives of a number of Korean males captured and transported to Japan during the Japanese invasions of 1592–1598.

The "Three T'ang Style-Poets"(Yi Tal, Paek Kwanghun, and Ch'oe Kyŏngch'ang) in the late sixteenth century scorned the complex rhetoric and difficult allusions—in short, court taste—and emphasized in their work the faithful expression of emotion that came from real-life experience. The period from the eighteenth century on saw the rise of practical learning scholars, a middle class, and commoners. They criticized Neo-Confucian ideology, drew vigorously upon vernacular literature, and searched for a new style. In his work, produced over eighteen years of exile, Chŏng Yagyong (1762–1836), for example, depicted the real life of farmers and fishermen by capturing regional detail. Based on a new understanding of the people and of Korean particularity, there appeared a "Chosŏn-style poetry" that criticized social contradictions, dealt with Korean history and natural features, and showed interaction with folk songs and poetry written for amusement (as in the work of Kim Sakkat, 1807–1863). From the middle class came countercultural voices that weakened the ruling elite's monopoly of literary life.

CH'OE CH'IWŎN (B. 857)

On a Rainy Autumn Night

I only chant painfully in the autumn wind,
For I have few friends in the wide world.
At third watch it rains outside.
By the lamp my heart flies myriad miles away.

CHŎNG CHISANG (D.1135)

Parting

After a rain on the long dike, grasses are thick.
With sad song I send you off to the South Bank.
When will the Taedong River cease to flow?
Year after year my tears will swell the waves.

YI ILLO (1152–1220)

Cicada

You drink wind to empty yourself,
Imbibe dewdrops to cleanse.
Why do you get up at autumn dawn
And keep crying so mournfully?

Night Rain on the Rivers Hsiao and Hsiang

A stretch of blue water between the shores in autumn:
The wind sweeps light rain over a boat coming back.
As the boat is moored at night near the bamboos,
Each leaf rustles coldly, awakening sorrow.

On the River on a Spring Day

High high azure peaks—a bundle of brush tips,
The broad river, far and hazy, spreads beyond the pines.
Files of dark clouds—an array of strange letters,
A vast blue sky—scroll of dispatch.

Written on the Wall of Ch'ŏnsu Monastery

I wait for a guest who does not come;
I look for a monk who is also out.
Only a bird[1] beyond the grove
Welcomes me, urging me to drink.

PL

1. The bird *t'i-hu* (K. *cheho*) is supposed to sing *t'i-hu t'i-hu*, which means to "take the pot for wine."

YI KYUBO (1168–1241)

Farmhouse: Three Poems

The village mill echoes
    though wispy smoke crisscrosses.
There are no walls along the length of the lane;
    clustered thorny trees are demarcators here.
Horses dot the mountain;
    cattle are scattered through the fields.
Everywhere I see the face
    of a great age of peace.

The loom importunes
    in the heavy frost and chill of dawn.
In the darkening smoke of the setting sun,
    the woodcutter sings as he returns.
How could an old countryman know
    the ninth day of the ninth month?
Yet he dips in his mellow wine
    those yellow chrysanthemums he chanced upon.

The leaves of the mountain pear are red,
    yellow the leaves of the mulberry.
Along the road the breeze returns,
    thick with the fragrance of rice stalks.
The sound of water being scooped from the well
    is echoed in the wooden clogs;
through the open brushwood gate
    moonlight carpets the frost.

Poetry: A Chronic Disease

I'm over seventy now,
an official of the first rank;
I know I should give up writing poetry,
but somehow I can't.
Mornings I sing like a cricket;
evenings I hoot like an owl.
I'm possessed by a devil I can't exorcise;
night and day it follows me stealthily around.
Once possessed, there's never a moment free;
a pretty mess it's got me in.
Day after day, I shrivel heart and liver
just to write a few poems.
Body fats and fluids depleted,
there's nothing left but skin and gristle.
Bones protruding, struggling to recite,
I strike a very foolish figure.
I have no words to elicit wonder,
nothing to pass on that will last a thousand years.
I clap my hands, guffaw, and when the laughing
     bout subsides, I begin to recite again.
My life and death hang on poetry;
not even a physician could cure this disease.

The Mad Rout of the Rat

My reason for raising a cat was not to catch you;
I had hoped the sight of the cat
     would make you cower and hide.
But you don't hide;
instead you bore through the walls,
     you come and go at will: why? why?
It's bad enough that you come out to play;
how dare you instigate this present mad rout!
Your squabbles are so raucous you interfere with sleep;
you steal our food with incredible speed.
The fact that you whizz around in spite of the cat
shows that the cat is lacking in skill.
The cat may not be doing its job,
but your crimes are weighty still.
I can whip the cat, I can drive it out,
but you are difficult to catch and tie.
Rats, rats, mend your ways
or I'll govern you with a fierce new cat.

How I Felt Pawning My Coat:
Shown to Ch'oe Chongbon

Third month, eleventh day;
no reason to light the kitchen fire this morning.
The wife said she'd pawn my fur;
I scolded her at first and stopped her.
I suppose the cold has already gone,
what pawnbroker would take the coat?
Suppose the cold returns,
how am I to survive the winter?
The wife retorted angrily:
how can you be so foolish?
I know that it's not the most glorious coat ever,
but the thread was woven by these hands;
I grudge it twice as much as you,
but mouth and belly are more urgent than furs.
A man who doesn't eat twice a day, the ancients say,
is heading for starvation,
and a starving man can drop morning or evening;
so how can you promise yourself another winter?
I called the servant and sent him at once to sell the fur.
I thought we'd survive for several days on the proceeds.
But what the servant brought back was no equivalent.
Suspicious, I suggested he might have pocketed some for himself.
The servant's face went an angry color.
He quoted the pawnbroker:
already summer encroaches on what's left of spring,
is it reasonable to buy furs at a time like this?
The only reason I'm willing to parry winter early

is that I have a little extra.
If I didn't have that bit to spare,
I wouldn't give you a single bag of grain.
Hearing this, I was ashamed, ashamed;
tears flowed down and wet my chin.
Fruit of arduous midwinter weaving,
given away in a morning,
brings no relief from great hunger;
famished children in a line like bamboo stalks.
I look back to younger, more sprightly days
when I knew nothing of the affairs of the world.
For a man who has read thousands of books, I thought,
passing the government examination
will be like pulling a hair from my beard.
I was filled with sudden self-conceit;
surely a good post will be allotted me.
Why have I had such a mediocre lot,
why has poverty embraced my sad path?
Reflecting sincerely on all this,
obviously I'm not without fault.
In my drinking, I never had control;
invariably I tipped a thousand cups.
Words normally kept hidden in my heart
under wine's influence were not held back.
I didn't stop till I had spewed everything out,
little knowing how false charges and vilification follow.
My conduct uniformly thus,
I deserved all this poverty and hunger.
Those beneath me did not like me,
heaven above denied me its protection.
Wherever I went, things got fouled up;
whatever I did turned out wrong.
All my own doing.
Sad, but who can I blame?
I counted my sins on my fingers
and gave myself three lashes of the whip.
But what's the point in repenting the past;
what I have to do is improve the future.

Burning My Manuscripts

In my youth I used to write songs.
When the brush moved down the page,
I wrote with unimpeded flow.
My poems, I thought, were as beautiful as jade;
who dared talk about flaws?
Afterwards, I studied them again:
there wasn't a fine word in one of them.
To retain them would be to soil my writing box:
unbearable thought, so I burned them in the kitchen fire.
If I look next year at this year's poems,
they will all be the same; I'll scrap them too.
Perhaps that's why Minister Kao of old
first composed when he was fifty.

Composed Playfully on New Year's Day

This body of mine has lived a lot of years;
I wonder where it has piled them though.
If I could put them in my pocket and count,
I'd empty them out, one by one, and hand them back to heaven.

The Moon in the Well

A monk coveted the moon in the well
And fished it up with water into a bottle.
But back at the temple, he will find
When the bottle tilts, the moon spills.

Thoughts on Eyes Growing Dim:
Presented to Chŏn Iji

I'm forty-four now;
both eyes are beginning to blur.
I can't distinguish people even at very close range;
it's as if a dense spring mist were blocking the view.
I consulted a physician. The physician said:
Your liver is the problem, it's not what it should be;
or perhaps when you were young,
you read too much in the shadow of the lamp.
Hearing this, I clapped my hands and laughed outright.
You're not a very skilled physician, I said.
People with ears want to hear;
those who can't hear are deaf.
People with eyes want to see;
those who can't see are blind.
I wanted to see the king,
but I had no access to the nine-gate palace.
I wanted to see men of rank in ceremonial cloth of gold,
but, dressed in hemp, I couldn't conceal my presence.
I wanted to see the peonies,
but only useless weeds grew verdant.
I never lived in a first-rate house;
in a hut in a mugwort field my hair turned white.
I never ate fine ceremonial food;
many's the time I missed a meal.
That's why my eyes are dim,
that's why they're bothering me as if veiled in hemp.
This is all the decree of heaven;

I can't cure it with medicine.
Who knows, it may turn out to be a blessing;
I may finish my days deaf and blind.

Grieving for My Little Girl

My little girl's face was white as snow;
I can't tell you how bright and intelligent she was.
She was talking by the time she was two,
her tongue more elastic than a parrot.
At three she became girl-conscious, reserved;
she didn't go outside the gate to play.
This year she was four; already she was good at sewing.
How could she be deprived of life,
how could she be gone to the other world?
It was all so sudden it's unreal:
a nestling fallen to the ground before it could grow,
a terrible indictment of her father's home.
I am acquainted with the Way;
I can bear my pain to a point,
but the tears of my wife, when will they end?
I look at the field:
new shoots beset by unseasonable wind and hail
face certain destruction.
The Creator put her here;
the Creator just as suddenly snatched her away.
What happens in this world is all subterfuge,
life's comings and goings are illusory.
It's all over now; go in peace to your eternal rest.

Sung Impromptu

Without wine I stop singing;
without song I'm averse to wine.
I delight in both wine and song;
they go together, they complement each other.
I trust my hand to compose a verse;
I trust my mouth to drink a cup.
Ah, what is an incorrigible man to do?
I've learned to enjoy both wine and song.
Wine never meant drinking a lot;
I couldn't keep up with a thousand songs.
Sitting face to face with a cup of wine brought on the mood;
I have no idea why this should be so.
As a result my sickness has grown progressively worse;
only with death will the habit be broken.
Thus it's not just me who gets upset;
those around me continually rebuke me.

On Poetry

Writing poetry is a consummate art;
expression and thought form a lovely harmony.
When thought's significance is truly deep
the flavor improves with every chew.
Deep thought without smooth expression
makes for coarse texture;
the unfolding of meaning is precluded.
Decorating and chiseling for embellishment
are of secondary importance,
and yet it takes a supreme effort
to reject a fine line not quite to the point.
To grab the flower and abandon the fruit
causes the poem to lose real meaning.
Today's crop of poets ignore
the profound worth of the *Book of Songs*.
They decorate the skin colorfully;
they follow the fashion of the moment.
Meaning is postulated in heaven;
it is hard to get it right.
Aware of this difficulty
they are content to decorate the exterior.
Thus they try to dazzle the crowd,
to conceal the absence of deep thought.
With the gradual development of this trend
good writing has been knocked to the ground.
Li Po and Tu Fu are not coming back;
on whose authority am I to sort
the true from the false?

I want to repair the broken base of letters,
but there's no one to carry a basket of earth.
I can recite three hundred verses from the *Book of Songs*;
whom can I satirize, whom can I help?
All I can do is do what I can.
I cry alone: others laugh me to scorn.

OR

YI CHEHYŎN (1287–1367)

After the Snow in the Mountains

The paper quilt grows cold, the temple light dim;
The novice has not rung a bell all through the night.
He will start grumbling if I open the door so early.
But I have to see the garden pine laden with snow.

CK

Contemporary Folk Songs

I carve a small rooster from wood
And pick it up with chopsticks and put it on the wall.
When this bird crows cock-a-doodle-do,
Then my mother's face will be like the setting sun.

***

At a wash place by the stream under a drooping willow,
Holding the hand of a handsome youth, I whispered.
Not even the March rain falling from the eaves
Could wash away his lingering scent on my fingertips!

***

A magpie chatters in a flowering bough by the hedge,
A spider spins a web above the bed.
Knowing my heart, they announce his return—
My beloved will be back soon.

***

Long ago in Silla, Venerable Ch'ŏyong
Is said to have emerged from the emerald sea.
With white teeth and ruddy lips he sang in the moonlight night,
And danced in a spring wind with square shoulders and purple
    sleeves.

PL

NATIONAL PRECEPTOR T'AEGO (1301–1382)

Nothingness

Still—all things appear.
Moving—there is nothing.
What is nothingness?
Chrysanthemums bursting in the frost.

On a Deathbed

Life is like a bubble—
Some eighty years, a spring dream.
Now I'll throw away this leather sack,
A crimson sun sinks on the west peak!

P L

SŎNG SAMMUN (1418–1456)

At the Execution Ground

The beating drum presses for my life;
I turn and see the sun is about to set.
No inn is provided by the underworld;
At whose house will I sleep tonight?

SŎNG KAN (1427–1456)

A Fisherman

Mountains rise over mountains and smoke from valleys;
The dust of the world can never touch the white gulls.
The old fisherman is by no means disinterested;
In his boat he owns the moon over the west river.

K I M   S I S Ŭ P (1435–1493)

Now Shine, Now Rain

Now shine, now rain, and rain becomes shine:
That is the sky's way as well as men's.
My glory may well lead to my ruin;
Your escape from fame will bring you a name.
Flowers may open or fall, but spring doesn't care;
Clouds will come and go, but mountains do not argue.
I tell you, men of the world, you must remember
Nowhere will you find happiness all your life.

CK

LINKED VERSE BY FIVE POETS (1442)

Upon Listening to the Flute

Where does it come from, the sound of a flute,
At midnight on a blue-green peak

Sŏng Sammun

Shaking the moonlight, it rings high,
Borne by the wind, it carries afar.

Yi Kae

Clear and smooth like a warbler's song,
The floating melody rolls downhill.

Sin Sukchu

I listen—a sad melody stirs my heart,
I concentrate—it dispels my gloom.

Pak P'aengnyŏn

Always, ever, a lover looks in the mirror,
And, amid vibrant silence, night deepens in the hills.

Yi Sŏkhyŏng

Splitting a stone, limpid notes are stout,
"Plucking a Willow Branch" breaks a lover's heart.[2]

Sŏng Sammun

Clear and muddy notes come in order,
The *kung* and *shang* modes unmixed.[3]

Yi Kae

2. A "Music Bureau" song accompanied by a horizontal flute; so is "Plum Blossoms Fall," nine lines later.
3. The first two notes of the pentatonic scale.

How wonderful, notes drawn out and released,
How pleasant, reaping waves of sound.

Sin Sukchu

Long since I played it seated on my bed.
Where is the zestful player leaning against the tower?

Pak P'aengnyŏn

Marvelous melodies recall Ts'ai Yen,[4]
Who remembers Juan Chi's clear whistle?[5]

Yi Sŏkhyŏng

"Plum Blossoms Fall" in the garden,
Fishes and dragons fight in the deep sea.

Sŏng Sammun

First, the drawn-out melody startled me,
Now I rejoice in the clear, sweet rhythm.

Yi Kae

How can only a reed whistle in Lung
Make the Tartar traders flee homesick?

Sin Sukchu

On Mount Kou-shih a phoenix calls limpidly,
In the deep pool a dragon hums and dances.

Pak P'aengnyŏn

A wanderer is struck homesick over the pass,
A widow pines in her room.

Yi Sŏkhyŏng

Floating, floating, the music turns sad,
Long, long, my thought is disquieted.

Sŏng Sammun

We were all ears at the first notes,
But can't grasp the dying sounds.

Yi Kae

A startled wind rolls away the border sands,
Cold snow drives through Ch'in Park.

Sin Sukchu

4. The daughter of Ts'ai Yung (133–192) and a skilled musician.

5. Juan Chi (210–263), a poet, musician, and lover of wine, one of the "Seven Worthies of the Bamboo Grove." Juan is known for his "Singing of Thoughts," comprising eighty-five poems.

I don't tire of your music,
Should I rise and dance to your tune?

Pak P'aengnyŏn

Who is that master flautist?
His creative talent is all his own.

Yi Sŏkhyŏng

Prince Ch'iao is really not dead,[6]
Has Huan I returned from the underworld?[7]

Sŏng Sammun

His solo—a whoop of a single crane,
In unison—a thousand ox-drawn carriages.

Yi Kae

Choking, choking, now a tearful complaint,
Murmuring, murmuring, now a tender whisper.

Sin Sukchu

I beg you, flute master,
Hide your art, don't spoil it.

Yi Sŏkhyŏng

Confucius heard Shao and lost his taste for meat;[8]
I too forget to take my meal.

Pak P'aengnyŏn

I cannot help cherishing your heart,
I set forth my deep love for you!

Sŏng Sammun

P L

6. Wang-tzu Ch'iao, or Wang-tzu Chin, Prince Ch'iao is said to have been a son of King Ling of Chou (sixth century B.C.), the noted player of the sheng (mouth organ made of thirteen bamboo pipes), who became a transcendent on Mount Kou-shih.

7. Huan I (d. c. 392) was a great flautist of the Chin.

8. *Analects* 7:13 and 3:25 (Waley, pp. 125 and 101). Waley translates Shao as "Succession Dance," which Confucius found to be perfect beauty.

KIM KOENGP'IL (1454–1504)

My Way

I live in peace and quiet, confining myself to home;
Only the moon is invited to shine on my loneliness.
Please do not ask me how I am getting along;
There are endless misty waves and hills on hills.

IM ŎNGNYŎNG (1496–1568)

To a Friend

At the gate of an old temple, another spring ends,
Sprinkling my clothes with petals and rain.
As I return, sleeves full of the sweet fragrance,
Mountain bees swarm after me from afar.

LADY SIN SAIMDANG (1504–1552)

Looking Homeward from a Mountain Pass

Leaving my old mother in the seaside town,
Alas! I am going alone up to Seoul.
As I turn, once in a while, to look homeward on my way,
White clouds rush down the darkening blue mountains.

CK

HWANG CHINI (C. 1506–1544)

Taking Leave of Minister So Seyang

In the moonlit garden paulownia leaves fall;
In the frost, wild chrysanthemums wither.
The tower is tall as the sky,
Drunk, we keep on draining our cups.
Flowing water is cold as the lute;
Plum fragrance seeps into my flute.
Tomorrow, after we have parted,
Our love will be green waves unending.

YI HYANGGŬM (1513–1550)

To a Drunken Guest

The drunken guest clings to my sleeve,
My gauze sleeve gets torn as I shake him off.
I don't mind the torn blouse,
I only fear the end of our love.

GREAT MASTER SŎSAN (1520–1604)

In Praise of the Portrait of My Former Master

Your white robes are made of white clouds,
Your blue pupils, strips of water.
Your stomach cradles precious gems,
Your heavenly light pierces the Big Dipper.

GREAT MASTER CHŎNGGWAN (1533–1609)

At the Moment of My Death

The three-foot-long sword that can split a feather
I've hidden in the Great Dipper.
In the great void no trace of clouds,
Now you see its sharp point!

P L

SONG IKP'IL (1534–1599)

Boating at Dusk

Lost among flowers, the boat returns late,
Expecting the moon, it drifts slowly down the shoals.
Though I am drunk, I still drop a line:
The boat moves on, but not my dream.

To the Moon

When on the wane, you are always impatient to wax,
But how so easily do you wane after waxing?
You are full only once in a month's thirty nights:
Man's mind in a lifetime is exactly the same.

SŎNG HON (1535–1598)

By Chance

Forty years I've lived in the green hills;
Who will pick a fight with me?
I sit alone in a hut with the spring breeze—
How idle laughing flowers and dozing willows!

CK

YI SUNSIN (1545–1598)

In the Chinhae Camp

By the sea the autumn sun sinks;
Startled by cold, the geese pitch a camp.
Anxious, I toss and turn—
Only a dawn moon on my bow and sword.

IM CHE (1559–1587)

A Woman's Sorrow

A beautiful girl, fifteen years old,
Too shy to speak, sends her lover away.
Back home, she shuts the double gate
And sobs before the pear blossoms.

Y U   M O N G I N   (1559–1623)

A Poor Woman

A poor woman at a shuttle, tears on her cheeks,
Weaves winter cloth for her husband.
Come morning, she tears a strip for a tax officer;
No sooner one leaves than another comes.

HŎ NANSŎRHŎN (1563–1589)

Poor Woman

Till her fingers are stiff with cold,
She cuts the cloth with scissors
To make a dress for a girl to be married:
But every year she keeps to her empty room.

PL

KWŎN P'IL (1569–1612)

Upon Reading Tu Fu's Poetry

The literary art of Tu Fu[9] is
   honored throughout the world.
Every time I open his works and read
   I feel a great life in spirits.
It's a divine wind murmuring,
   born in deep ravines,
Heavenly music pealing out,
   sounded by an ancient bell,
A speeding hawfinch crossing an azure sky
   after clouds have cleared,
A herd of dragons sporting in a blue sea
   when the moon is bright.
As before, setting out on a road
   to mountains where an immortal dwells,
I savor a thousand peaks
   and then ten thousand more.

RL

9. Known as the "Sage of Poetry," Tu Fu (712–770) is generally considered the greatest poet in the Chinese language. His well-wrought personal and social poems have been studied and admired.

At the Grave of Chŏng Ch'ŏl

Leaves fall with rain in these vacant mountains;
Silent is the graceful voice of the poet-official.
Alas! I cannot offer you a cup this morning;
You had a song that foretold it, in the old days.

CK

CHO HWI (FL. 1568–1608)

In Peking to a Woman with a Veil

Shy, you veil your face on the street—
Clear moonlight through faint clouds.
Your slender waist, tightly bound, is a handspan,
Your new gauze skirt a pomegranate color.

YI TAL (FL. 1568–1608)

Mountain Temple

A temple buried in white clouds—
But monks do not sweep them away.
A guest comes, the gate opens;
In every valley, yellow pine pollen.

GREAT MASTER CHUNGGWAN (FL. 1590)

Upon Reading Chuang Tzu[10]

Give me wings, I'll reach a high heaven,
With scales I can dive into a deep pool.
How silly, you dreamer within a dream,
Not knowing your body's in a melting furnace.

PL

10. Chuang Tzu (355?–275 B.C.) is a Taoist thinker, whose work with the same name contains many enlightening and entertaining stories.

YUN SŎNDO (1587–1671)

At My Study

My eyes fixed on the mountains and my ears on the zither,
How could affairs of the world ever disturb my mind?
Though nobody knows I am full of lively spirits,
Wildly I sing out a song and then intone it alone.

CK

KIM CH'ANGHYŎP (1651–1708)

Mountain Folk

I dismount and ask, "Anybody home?"
A housewife emerges from the gate.
She seats me under the eaves
And fixes a meal for the guest.
"Where is your husband?" I ask.
"Up the hill at dawn with a plow."
It must be hard to furrow the hill;
He isn't back even after sunset.
Not a single soul around,
Only chickens and dogs on tiered slopes.
"In the woods there are tigers,
I can't fill my basket with greens."
"What makes you live alone
Among rugged paths in the valley?"
"I know life is easier on the plain,
But I am afraid of the king's men."

PL

CH'OE KINAM (SEVENTEENTH CENTURY)

Elegy to Myself

I have never had my fill even of poor food.
So how could I hope for dishes and cups on my death?
I have never had more than a mugful of drink,
So how should I expect to taste a morsel of meat?
I go out the gate of the capital city
To lie beneath the west hill in the field.
The wind in the forest sobs in sorrowful sounds;
The moon over the hills beams its sad light.
The world is a place for a short stay:
My real home is in the underworld.
Who knows if the joy of a skeleton
Will go on and on, like heaven and earth?

CK

NǓNGUN (DATES UNKNOWN)

Waiting for My Love

He said he would come at moonrise;
The moon is out, but he has not come.
Perhaps he lives among high hills
Where the moon comes up late.

PL

CHŎNG YAGYONG (1762–1836)

Laughing at Myself

You may have grain, but nobody to eat it,
And worry about hunger if you have sons.
When you're promoted, you must become fool,
While the talented cannot find a place.
A household can seldom enjoy perfect bliss,
And the best principles always collapse.
A miserly father has always a prodigal son,;
An intelligent wife a stupid husband.
When the moon is full, clouds often come;
When flowers bloom, the wind often blows.
This is the way of things.
So I laugh by myself, but nobody knows.

CK

KIM PYŎNGYŎN (1807–1863)

A Song for My Shadow

You follow me as I come and go,
    No one is more polite than you,
You are like me,
    But you are not I.
On the shore under a setting moon
    Your giant shape startled me;
In the courtyard under midday sun
    Your small pose makes me laugh!
I try to find you on my pillow,
    But you are not there;
When I turn around in front of my lamp,
    We suddenly meet again.
Although in my heart I love you,
    I cannot trust you after all—
When no light is there to shine,
    You leave without a trace!

RL

HWANG O (NINETEENTH CENTURY)

The Swing

The girl, fourteen years old but bigger than me,
Has learned to swing like a swallow flying.
As I dare not speak aloud from outside her window,
I scribble on a persimmon leaf and throw it to her.

CK

PYŎN WŎNGYU (FL. 1881)

To a Friend

Day after day I live, deer for company,
Bright moon on the waters and clouds on the hills.
Nothing except these in the crevice of my heart—
Shall I send you a painting of autumn sound?

PL

HWANG HYŎN (1855–1910)

On Killing Myself

Growing old through all these turbulent years,
I have often come very close to ending my life.
But today truly I have no other choice:
A flaring candle lights up the dark blue sky.

CK

FOLK SONGS

Korean folk songs began to be collected systematically from the twentieth century. The lyrics of some folk songs were recorded earlier in such works as the *Memorabilia of the Three Kingdoms* (1285) in hyangch'al orthography and Yi Chehyŏn's "A Small Collection of Folk Songs" (*So akpu*), but in Chinese. Folk songs sung in the thirteenth and fourteenth centuries, such as those preserved in *Words for Songs and Music* and *Notations for Korean Music in Contemporary Use*, were recorded in the Korean alphabet in compilations dating from the early sixteenth century. Those from the Chosŏn period appear not to be very different from those that are sung today. After the 1930s scholars of Korean literature began collecting folk songs in a concerted effort to preserve indigenous Korean culture.[1] A project undertaken by the Academy of Korean Studies resulted in the compilation of some six thousand songs from all over the country (1984).

Folk songs are sung to the tasks of daily life. Often they serve to coordinate the rhythm of communal chores. Those who lash and flail must take turns in threshing barley, for example, and singing a song allows the workers to mesh their efforts and work smoothly together. Such a phenomenon emerges all the more clearly in cases where several people must join strength to accomplish a certain task together. In grinding grain, or laying the foundations of houses, several people must pull on a rock together or pack the soil. In such cases work songs serve the practical function of signaling the beginning and end of certain movements.

1. Kim Soun (b. 1902) published *Chōsen minyōshū* (Collection of Korean folk songs) in 1929 (Tokyo: Taibunkan), *Chōsen minyōsen* (Selections of Korean folk songs) in 1933 (Tokyo: Iwanami shoten) in Japanese, and *Chosŏn kujŏn minyo chip* (Collection of Korean folk songs) in Korean in 1933 (Tokyo: Daiichi shobō).

A secondary function of work songs is to ease the physical toil and boredom of the task by providing amusement. Weeding, woodcutting, weaving, and sewing do not demand a great output of energy at any particular moment, but they do require continued effort over a prolonged period of time. By coordinating the motion to the rhythm of the music, workers can enhance the efficiency of the work and simultaneously ease the boredom caused by repetition. Some folk songs, such as the pallbearer's dirge or the song of pounding the soil when a burial mound is prepared, are necessary in conducting rituals as well.

Play songs are sung in the process of conducting play activities. When people gather for these activities, play songs can serve as instructions for certain motions just as work songs do for certain tasks. Representative of this genre is "Kang kang sullae" from the southwestern coast of South Chŏlla province.

Folk songs without specific functions are sung simply for fun. Songs without function in one part of the country, however, may be sung for specific purposes in another. "Arari," for example, is sung in Yŏju county of Kyŏnggi province when transplanting rice seedlings.

"Arirang," which exists in regionally distinctive versions, is considered the representative folk song of Korea. "Arirang" typically starts with a refrain announcing that it is being sung: "Arirang arirang arariyo." The sentiment at the heart of "Arirang" is the sorrow of parting. The feelings of hurt, wounded pride, reproach, and resentment at the betrayal of a loved one are mixed together. The desire for the return of the loved one and the reversal of parting are expressed humorously. Such a sentiment of parting forms one strand of tradition running through classical Korean poetry, and "Arirang," together with other similar songs dealing with the same theme, are sung mostly from the perspective of the woman, portraying the loneliness of a life lived in the absence of the loved one.

Folk songs are expressions of the everyday feelings that inform common people's lives. Work songs in particular express in a straightforward fashion, without embellishments, the humble joy and sense of reward that farmers and workers experience as they work, as in "Transplanting Young Rice Plants." The pain and hardship marking the life of the commonfolk also find expression in folk song. Various songs that deal with the life of a woman at the in-laws describe the difficulties a young woman goes through after marriage. Transplanted to an unfamiliar and often hostile environment where she occupies the lowest place in the domestic hierarchy, the newly married woman must endure an endless cycle of physical work, undernourishment, and psychological abuse. In "Wretched Married Life," after extreme mistreatment that includes being forced to weed fields under the burning sun without lunch, a young woman runs away from her husband's family and becomes a Buddhist nun. The song reflects the abuses of patriarchal Chosŏn society from the perspective of the victim.

Transplanting Song

MEN: O girl picking cotton in a long dense field,
I'll pick cotton and cotton ball for you,
So let's pledge a marriage bond.
O girl picking lotus leaves at Konggal pond in Sangju,
I'll pick lotus seeds and wild rice for you,
So let's pledge a marriage bond.

WOMEN: Where has the idle owner gone after planting seedlings?
He left no trace but went to his concubine
Whose room is a flowerbed, while the wife's is a lotus pond.

MEN: Leaving this sluice gate and that in disrepair,
Where has the idle owner gone?
He went to his concubine's with tobacco and gifts.

WOMEN: What kind of a woman is she that
He goes to her day and night?
During the days to play and nights to sleep.

MEN: No trees in Seoul, they made bridges with hairpins.

WOMEN: Crossing this bridge and that
Makes me dance naturally.

WOMEN: In a bamboo grove in Seoul,
White doves laid their eggs.
If you give me this egg and that,
I can take the civil service exam.

MEN: The sun rising over the eastern hill
        Crosses the western hill at dusk.

WOMEN: Where is my beloved gone?
        He does not know it's supper time.

MEN: "O birds, birds, mandarin ducks,
        Where do you come from after sleep?"
        "I slept on the green willow, swaying this way and that."

WOMEN: In a loft in Yu's home in Seoul,
        A golden dove laid eggs.
        If you give me this egg and that,
        I can take the civil service exam this year.

WOMEN: I go on a horseback to a prison.
        "Open the door, jailer, I'm here to see my brothers."

MEN: Where is that bier going at sunset?
        It's the bier carrying Li Po's wife.

WOMEN: At sunset I look back at the half-moon over the paddy.
        Not a half-moon but a moon of the first days.
        O love, my love, handsome as a silk lantern,
        You left me alone and went to Seoul.
        He returns, returns, being carried
        On a coffin board with seven holes.
        Where is the dead gone?
        Only a hemp banner marking the funeral.

MEN: O silk lantern, blue silk lantern,
        Light the beloved's room brightly.
        We're in bed, so who will turn off the light?

MEN: The sun rising over the eastern hill
        Crosses the western hill at dusk.
        A shadow looms over the valley.
        Where is my love—she does not know it's supper time.

WOMEN: The sun has set, an early moon over the paddy.
It's not a half-moon but a moon of the first days.

MEN: The sun has set, the day is gone,
A shadow looms over the valley.
Where is my love—she does not know it's supper time.

WOMEN: Motley jacket sewn with a medium needle—
I put ribbons on a buckle.
You promised it to me, so give it now,
Don't give it so late.

MEN: Pretty gentle girl sitting on a mulberry tree—
I'll pick mulberry leaves and lotus seeds,
So let's pledge a marriage bond.

WOMEN: I want, I want, I want to put on an Ulp'o blouse.
Look at her breast round like a round compact.

WOMEN: I'll buy you shoes, I'll buy you a pair of maiden shoes.
They'll find out if you get an uncommon pair.
If you give me money, I'll fall in love with you.

WOMEN: A bowl of flour dough on the son-in-law's tray—
Where is my daughter gone like a thief,
Leaving her mother alone to worry?

Wretched Married Life
(Folk Song from Koch'ang)

On the third day of my marriage,
My in-laws asked me to weed a field
With a hoe made of wood.
When I reached the field,
It was hot as fire, and
The field was long as a ridgeline.
But I weeded three furrows.
When lunchtime came,
Everyone's lunch was brought.
But no one brought mine for me.
When I entered my so-called home
And stood before the big gate,
My father-in-law asked,
"Daughter-in-law, daughter-in-law,
How many furrows have you weeded?"
"On a day hot as fire,
I've weeded three furrows
Of a long and stony field.
Everyone's lunch was brought
Except for mine."
"You wretched woman, get out!
You call that work
And ask for a meal?"
When I reached the middle of the courtyard.
My husband's younger brother asked,
"Aunt, aunt, how many furrows did you weed?"
"On a day hot as fire,
I've weeded three furrows

Of an arid and stony field.
But no one brought me lunch."
"You wretched woman, you call that work
And ask for lunch when lunchtime comes?"
When I stepped up from the courtyard,
My sister-in-law asked,
"Sister-in-law, sister-in-law,
How many furrows have you weeded?"
"I've weeded three furrows
Of a long and stony field,
But no one brought me lunch."
"You wretched woman, go away,
You call that work and ask
For lunch when lunchtime comes?"
When I entered the kitchen,
My mother-in-law, holding a rice paddle, asked,
"Daughter-in-law, daughter-in-law,
How many furrows have you weeded?"
"On a day hot as fire,
I've weeded three furrows
Of a long and stony field.
Everyone else's lunch was brought,
But no one brought mine."
"Wretched woman, you call that work
And ask for lunch when time comes!"
What they gave me to eat was
Year-old boiled barley
With a year-old soy sauce.
What they called a spoon was
A spade for scooping dung
At Scholar Chŏng's house.
Even that she did not just give
But threw it at me, and I ran to pick it up
And ate what you call a "meal."
An old woman in the neighborhood
Came to the kitchen and said,
"The world under heaven is earth,
So is earth in the underworld.
Have you really no place to live

Except for this household?"
I filled the crock with water
And told my mother-in-law:
"Mom, I am leaving,
I'm going to a temple."
"Hey, wretch! Go if you want.
My son can live without you."
I approached the male quarters
And told my father-in-law:
"I'm leaving, Dad,
I'm going to a temple."
"Hey, wretch! Go if you want;
My son can live without you."
I went to my room and opened
The chest made of beech wood,
Cut a piece from my eight-strip skirt
To fashion a peaked monk's hat,
Used the rest for a pair of trousers and blouse.
Donning the peaked hat and,
Carrying a knapsack on my back,
I went out into the courtyard:
"Listen, listen, father-in-law. Listen,
I'm going to a temple.
Listen, mother-in-law, too,
I'm going to a temple.
Sister-in-law, listen,
I'm going to a temple.
If your brother returns from Seoul,
Tell him I went to a temple."
So somehow I bid them farewell
And climbed to a temple with twelve gates.
I approached the first gate
And opened the door to the first room
Filled with young monks.
"Please shave my head, please."
"We can't do it for fear of gossip."
I opened the door to the second room
Filled with middle-aged monks.
"Please shave my head, please."

"We can't do it for fear of gossip."
I opened the door to the third room
Filled with old monks.
"Please shave my head, please."
"We can't do it for fear of gossip."
"When I am at this strait,
There will be no trouble,
So please shave my head."
I held a lamp in my hand, and
One monk shaved a side behind my ear.
My nun's robe was wet from tears.
I held a lamp with my hand,
And another shaved both sides of my head;
I could not weep loud.
"Oh, listen, people in the world,
Is there no place for me to live
Under the sky without pillars,
That I've my head shaved
With a young woman's face?"
After managing to pass three years
I the nun climbed a hill and saw
A gentleman approaching
Who looked like my own husband.
That gentleman said,
"Wouldn't there be a person like me
If you walked the four quarters?"
Looked at from the side it was he,
Looked at crossways it was he.
He was my man no matter how I looked,
It was clear that he was my husband.
I asked him to remove his hat—
Indeed, he was my husband!
Look how he behaved!
He dismounted from his horse in stockinged feet,
Rushed toward me, grasped my hands,
Examined my face, and exclaimed,
"What's happened, what's happened?
What has happened to my wife?"
"I won't go back to your household.

Don't speak nonsense, I won't return.
Now that I've had my head shaved,
I'll return after three years of study.
If it's only between you and me,
I'll go with you this instant:
But I cannot stand, not at all,
My father-in-law's yelling,
Mother-in-law's bitching,
And sister-in-law's chattering.
So I won't go with you.
Return to your home alone and marry
A girl like a flower from a good family.
When you enjoy the company of gallant men,
Don't forget even in a dream my pitiful life,
Don't forget how I've suffered.
If you think of me in your dream,
Then, even if I'm dead,
I'll tie grass to return your kindness."[2]

Parting from her like this,
The husband returned home.
His father came forward and said,
"Our daughter-in-law fled last night
Because you did not return."
The husband stopped taking food and water,
Entered the thatched hut in the rear garden,
And opened the door to her room.
Three feet of dust had settled.
A quilt, pillow, mandarin-duck embroidered bedding
Meant for two, a chamber pot,
A silver ring like a halter—
All scattered all over the room.
Where was the husband gone,
Not knowing how her innards burned?
If her father was a pharmacist,

2. Wei Ko of Chin, whose kindness in marrying his father's favorite concubine
to save her from burial with her husband's corpse was later rewarded when her
father tied grass knots to impede Wei's enemies in battle.

Would he be able to cure her illness?
Where was his wife gone,
When could he return her kindness?
At last he died of heartache,
And that household became
A field of mugwort abandoned.[3]

PL

3. The ending is ambiguous. It can also refer to the wife, who died of illness. I have combined several incomplete versions of the song so that it makes sense in English.

Chŏngsŏn Arirang

Will it snow, or will it rain?
Is the rainy season settling in?
On Mansu Mountain the dark clouds gather close.

Arirang, arirang, arariyo.
Let me cross Arirang hill.[4]

Sweetbrier, let it bloom on the long, beautiful sand beach.
Cuckoos, let them sing when March is fully spring.

The cuckoo on South Mountain sings, "Better go home, better
    go home."
It laments being far away from home.

Though I am wrapped in a hemp cloth skirt,
you, Mr. High Collar, do not impress me.

Hibiscus, not blooming for thirty-six years,
burst into blossom again at Liberation.

A porcelain bowl breaks in two or three pieces,
but if the Thirty-Eighth breaks, we become one.

If time wants to go, why not go on alone
instead of taking our brief youth?

4. Refrains omitted from stanza 2.

You teen-aged boys, don't laugh at gray hairs.
It won't be long before yours turn too.

I built a castle of thorns to block gray hairs,
but they arrived before I knew it.

River waters flow and flow, to settle into the sea.
My body that turns round and round, I wonder where it goes.

Your lot and mine are not blessed with blankets and bed,
so let us find the pleasures of a long straw mat.

Green shade, fragrant plants return year after year.
Why does my lover depart and not return?

Solitary gulls turn above Choyang River.
Without my love, my body turns round and round in my room.

South Mountain's mist wraps around its sides.
My lover's arms are bound around my waist.

Seeing the flash of the cigarette, I thought he had returned.
Miserable fireflies! You break my heart.

Good or bad, married life depends on luck.
Do not blame the matchmaker.

Ginseng, deer antlers are no use
for this husband-inflicted illness.

If you think of me as I do of you,
azaleas will bloom in cold December.

The old field across was not planted last year.
It stands unused another year, just like me.

Brother can wait until next year.
Sell the calf and marry me off.

The sun setting over the western hills does not leave because it
    wants to.
My lover too does not leave because he wishes.

I cried so much at your leaving, in such distress,
Songjŏng ferry crossing has become a Han River.

Chŏngsŏn's water mill spins with the stream through the
    seasons.
My husband does not know how to spin with me.

No rain falling on dry sand,
no sleep in my baby-husband's embrace.

Do you think we don't eat rice and beef because we don't know
    the taste?
Corn in any season is good enough if we are at peace.

If you don't like an A-frame to go with your hanging belly,
you will be a beggar and nothing more for a hundred years.

Keep this story to yourselves, sisters.
It is I who built the nest hidden in the hemp field.

On Fore South Mountain the woodpeckers drill brand-new
    holes.
Why can't my useless fool drill in a hole already made?

Kangwŏn's Kŭmgang Mountain has twelve thousand peaks
and eight thousand shrines,
but, instead of building a shrine on each peak
and praying there for money,
let us work together and build our own success.

D M

SHAMANIST NARRATIVE SONGS

A shamanist myth unique to Korea, "Song of Entertaining the Holy One" (*Sŏngin nori p'unyŏm*) tells of the union of a man and woman, conception, and birth, and share several motifs with foundation myths in the north such as those of Tangun and Chumong. In this agricultural myth the heroine's name is Tanggŭm aegi, *tan* being an ancient word meaning village or valley, and *kam* meaning god—hence a village/valley goddess who controls a space where human beings live. The hero, a monk, impregnates a woman, an act unbecoming of him, but he is still worshiped. The monk travels between the two worlds, earth and heaven, sharing characteristics of the heavenly god. His abode is on Heavenly God (Hwanggŭm) Mountain, a corrupt version of *han* (heavenly, great) and *kam* (god). Originally a heavenly god, the monk was metamorphosed into a Buddhist master after the introduction of Buddhism.

Also known as *Chesŏk ponp'uri* (*Tanggŭm aegi*), this shamanist narrative song exists in some fifty versions but has these central motifs: A certain noble family has nine sons and one daughter; for unavoidable circumstances, the family goes away, leaving only the daughter; an eminent monk from the West comes and asks for alms; while the daughter offers him alms, the monk impregnates her and leaves; upon returning home, the family learns of the daughter's pregnancy and drives her out; the daughter seeks out the monk who bestows priesthood on three sons she bore, and she herself becomes a deity. Variations lie primarily in the process of the daughter's conception, the manner of punishment, and the way the three sons obtain priesthood. The version presented here belongs to the northeast region and comes from Kanggye in North P'yŏngan province.

This text was first collected by Son Chint'ae (b. 1900) in July 1933 in Kanggye from a male shaman named Chŏn Myŏngsu. The text is usually recited at a major shamanist ritual to please and entertain the gods with food, wine, dance, and music. In this version the hero is Chujae Munjang, and the heroine is called Sŏjang aegi. The source is Sŏ Taesŏk and Pak Kyŏngjin, eds., *Sŏsa muga* (Seoul: Koryŏ taehakkyo Minjok munhwa yŏnguso, 1996), pp. 33–55. For a different version in prose see Peter H. Lee, ed., *Myths of Korea* (Somerset and Seoul: Jimoondang International, 2000), pp. 70–115.

Song of Entertaining the Holy One

The origin of the Holy One is Heavenly God Mountain,
The abbot of a temple on Heavenly God Mountain,
The Thus Come One Śākyamuni Buddha,
Yellow, white, and black holy images of buddhas.
The Holy One's mother is Prince Maŭl's wife,
His father is the scholar-prince Maŭl.
He proposed in the first year, then received a reply,
And in the third year they were married,
But grieved they had no child in the next three years.
One day a monk came to the east of a knotweed grove
And invoked the Bodhisattva Who Observes the Sounds of the
    World
And repeatedly recited the six-syllable prayer
Namo Amitābha, Homage to Amitābha.
Then the Holy One's mother looked out
And saw that he was no ordinary monk.
She went to the crock storing rice
And scooped up three *toe* and three *hop* of best-quality rice.
"O monk, listen to my story.
Please take this rice and officiate
At the feast of land and water and
In your prayer remember especially the one
Who cannot have a child."
The monk replied:
"If one could have a child with this puny offering,
 No one in the world would be childless.
Please, go up to Heavenly God Mountain
And offer sincere prayers for a hundred days."

So she decided to garner merit, and
With thirty-three *mal*, three *toe*, three *hop* of rice,[1]
Dishes fried with oil and made of radish,
Climbed the mountain and began her prayers.
Days she offered the feast of land and water,
Nights she lit candles and lanterns.
Thus she lit lanterns for a hundred days,
But even after ninety-nine days no response came.
So Prince Maŭl and his wife conferred:
"Our prayers have brought no result.
Let's descend after tonight's sleep."
At the first watch they fell asleep,
At the second watch they had a dream,
At the third watch they realized that
A red pearl came down from heaven
And landed on the princess's skirt.
The princess spoke to her husband:
"A red pearl from heaven landed on my skirt.
I don't know whether it's a good or bad dream."
The prince answered, "I don't know either."
So they returned home.
From that month on she had signs of pregnancy—
One month, two months, three and four months . . .
Blood gathered in the fifth, after nine months
The gates were closed, and in the ninth month
She gave birth to a son.
The baby spoke from inside the womb:
"I cannot emerge from your bottom.
Please take your gold hairpin with phoenix design
And draw a line across your belly
So that I can come out to the world."
She did so and the child emerged.
He looked earnestly for his father and mother
But could not speak from that day
Until he reached the age of thirteen.
He said, "Please make a knapsack from your skirt,

1. Units of measure: one *toe* makes ten *hop*. One *mal* is equivalent to about 18
liters.

A monk's cap from your inside sash,
And a monk's robe from Father's gown.
Then I will climb Heavenly God Mountain
And obtain my family name."
The princess was delighted that he spoke
And made a cap and robe for him.
Cap and robe on, shouldering a knapsack,
When viewed from front, he is a monk,
But from behind, he is a transcendent.
He reached the mountain and saw
Three buddhas sitting,
White buddha above,
Black buddha below,
And yellow buddha in the center.
The abbot on Heavenly God Mountain asked the buddhas,
"Please, give him his real name."
The white iron buddha answered,
"What shall I give for the family name?
I will give a knapsack for alms."
The black iron buddha asked "What shall I give?
I'll give a six-ring staff."
The yellow iron buddha asked, "What shall I give?
I'll give a wooden bell with a clapper."

When the abbot on Heavenly God Mountain
Came down with his real family name,
He heard a rumor about a certain man
Who lived well but was greedy,
Who would box the ear of a monk and drive him out,
Or smash the beggar's bowl,
Loan a grain with the outside of the measure,
And make one pay with the inside.
Intoning the six-syllable prayer,
The abbot asked him to offer rice.
The man spoke:
"That monk is no ordinary monk.
Wife, go out and offer him some rice."
Look how the wife behaved:
She carried a broken dipper and stumped broom,

Entered a storehouse three years old
And swept this corner and that
And gathered and offered a bowl of dust.
The abbot on Heavenly God Mountain
Received it and let a whirlwind remove straws,
Leaving only four mouse droppings.
He rubbed one dropping into a horse,
Another into a millipede,
The remaining two into a backpack frame[2]
And loaded them on the horse and came out.
The rich man looked out and saw that
The abbot was stealing all his fortune.
He asked his son to get them back,
But the son returned with four mouse droppings.
"If we leave them we will lose them,
So let's swallow them."
So the rich man's family sat around—
He swallowed one, his wife another,
His son the third, and daughter-in-law the fourth.
When the abbot was about to leave,
The daughter-in-law went to the crock
And scooped out three toe and three hop of rice.
The abbot took it and said as he left,
"Tomorrow at the Hour of the Horse,[3]
Your house will turn into a lotus pond."
"How sad!" The daughter-in-law asked,
"O monk, is there a way for us to survive?"
The abbot replied," If you trace my path, you'll live."
"How could I know where you went?"
"The path I take is where stones broke,
Soil was dug, trees fell—these will indicate the road I took.
Even if lightning strikes, never look back!"
"I'll abide," replied the daughter-in-law.
Then the abbot left. The following morning
The daughter-in-law went to the kitchen to cook.
From the four corners water gushed out,

2. Two frame sticks of a pack saddle.
3. Between 11 A.M. and 1 P.M.

The iron ridge of the roof gathered rust,
A six-yard-long snake crawled in,[4]
Looking back at the adjoining vegetable field.
So she went to her mother-in-law's bedroom and said:
"Mom, water is gushing out from the kitchen corners."
Mother-in-law answered:
"Don't scoop up the water on the surface,
But from inside, and cook rice and serve Dad."
"I found a pair of goldfish in the crock."
"When we set up our household,
Whenever we saw side dishes
We would call them thieves;[5]
But now that I'm getting old,
Catch and cook them as a side dish."
"The snake glancing at the field came in."
"Ah, when it's hot, you cannot go outside;
Maybe the heat drove it in.
A commoner became a daughter-in-law
Of a literary family, and
You chat with me instead of cooking.
Go to the kitchen and prepare the meal."
The stream water from the kitchen corners
Now flooded the floor, stones supporting the stove,
And the outer room. "We must leave."
A baby on her back and with a dog and cat,
A sewing basket on her head,
She traced the path taken by the abbot
And climbed the rear hill.
Suddenly lightning struck with heavy rain.
The abbot warned not to look behind
No matter how deafening the sound.
But she could not help peeping under her armpit,
And her whole house became a lotus pond;
Willow sprouted in the middle,
Her mother-in-law turned into a hen,
Her father-in-law into a cock;

4. The original has three spans (*pal*) of both arms.
5. Because they made them eat more rice.

They fluttered their wings and crowed
But fell from the tree and died.
They then became frogs, green and yellow,
And fought with each other.
From then on the frog's hand resembled the human's,
All because of the daughter-in-law's peep.
She then turned into a stone buddha.
From then on, rocks in the shape of a baby,
A basket, a dog, and a cat—these received food
Cooked with oil used on the eighth day of the fourth month,
And dishes made of turnip.
Leaving the place, the abbot came down to Sŏjang-aegi's;[6]
And when he reached her home with ninety-nine gates,
He opened the first, then the second,
And then the twelfth gate.
He opened it and entered the garden,
Reciting from the scriptures and
Offering the six-syllable prayer.
Sŏjang-aegi looked out and ordered the servant to offer rice.
The abbot said, "I'll refuse it if offered by the servants
But accept it only from Sŏjang-aegi."
Aegi said, "What a strange monk!" and herself scooped up
Three toe three hop of rice from the crock
And emptied it into the abbot's knapsack.
But the knapsack had a hole
And rice scattered all over the garden.
Aegi called the servant to bring a broom and winnow.
Then the abbot spoke:
"I can't eat rice swept from the yard and winnowed.
If Aegi herself gives it to me, I'll depart."
So Aegi and the abbot both gathered the rice—
Aegi two toe two hop and the abbot one toe one hop,
And the work was finished by sunset.
The abbot then said because it was getting dark
He would like to spend the night there.
Aegi answered, "Men are out, so you cannot."

6. The proper noun *aegi* means "baby" and "dear," when used as a diminutive
affective.

The abbot asked, "How about an open shed?"
Aegi answered, "You may sleep there."
When in the shed the abbot said,
"I'm afraid of the fodder chopper."
Aegi then suggested the servant's room.
The abbot opened the door, stepped one foot in,
But said he could not sleep there.
Aegi asked why he could not sleep there.
The abbot answered that it smelled of spittle.
"Then how about my older brother's room?"
The abbot opened the door, stepped one foot in,
But said he could not sleep there either.
Aegi asked why he could not sleep there.
The abbot answered because of the sound of yelling.
"How about the veranda leading to your bedroom?"
Aegi replied it was out of the question.
The abbot suggested, "What if you seal the door
Of your bedroom from inside and lock it,
Seal it and lock it?
If I enter the room without unlocking the door,
Then would you let me sleep there?"
Aegi thought he could not possibly open a locked door,
So consented and sealed the door from both sides.
The abbot was gone, however, with no trace.
Aegi thought she had been harassed for nothing,
Opened the door, entered her room,
And found the abbot already inside.
He hung up his robe on a peg Aegi used for her skirt,
His cap where she hung her hairpiece.
When Aegi did not know what to do, the abbot spoke to her:
"Bring wet sand and a bucketful of water,
Place them between you and me,
You sleep on the spot nearest to the fireplace,
I on the farthest spot from the fireplace.
The river is a thousand tricents wide,[7]

7. Tricent (three hundred paces): *ri*, a third of a mile, a suggestion made by
Victor H. Mair, *The Columbia Anthology of Traditional Chinese Literature* (New York:
Columbia University Press, 1994), p. xxxii.

So there will be no problem."
So they did as he proposed.
Both watched each other and dozed on and off.
The abbot then threw three fistfuls of sleep at Aegi.
At the first watch she began to sleep;
At the second watch she began to dream;
At the third watch she realized that
Three red pearls came down from heaven
And landed in front of her skirt.
She woke up—it was daybreak.
Emerging from her room she decided to divine
Her fortune with the shamans Chiha and Ch'ŏnha.
The abbot spoke: "I'll solve your dream for you.
Three red pearls from heaven means
You will soon have three sons.
Aektu Bodhisattva sitting on your right shoulder
And Kŭmdu Bodhisattva on your left
Indicate babies dawdling, and when they're born,
They will come to me for their family name."
The abbot gave Aegi a grain of rice
And asked her to prepare the morning meal.
Aegi wondered how she could cook a single grain
But thought, "He will find out if I add more."
So she put it in a cauldron and lit the fire.
The rice cooked by itself, and
Aegi brought a cauldron full.
The abbot, however, did not lift the lid.
She asked why and the abbot answered,
"We receive offerings by smell and taste by light.
We do not eat, but you may."
She found rice sweeter than any viands and dainties,
So she ate all but was not full.
She even ate scorched rice from the bottom.
While eating, the abbot was gone without a trace.
From that month on, Aegi showed signs of pregnancy.
Her rice and sauce began to taste bitter,
She asked only for wild grapes and garlic,
Began to be big with child,
And could not rise from the bed.

Aegi's father was on his way home
From his post in the province
And his return was announced with a gunshot.
Everyone but Aegi went out to greet him.
Her mom asked why Aegi had not come out,
And was told that the daughter was big with child.
Her mom scolded women servants
For slandering Aegi's good name
And herself went to find out.
Sure enough, she was big with child.
Aegi's dad exclaimed:
"What a calamity for a family of the ruling elite!
Go and fetch her at once!"
Servants went to bring her out,
But she said she would come by herself.
Look how she behaved:
Her right hand held a bamboo staff,
Her left hand a willow staff,
Her shoes worn wrong end up,
Her skirt upside down.
Aegi's dad ordered:
"Quickly put her head on the block!"
And to the executioner: "Behead her fast!"
The executioner's sword struck her neck
But broken into pieces, turning into
White and yellow butterflies
Fluttering among white clouds.
At this time the sword fell in front of the abbot,
Who examined it and said: "I must rescue her."
So his power stopped her from being killed.
Her father then ordered:
"Bind her hands from behind and attach a stone
And throw her into the lotus pond."
Aegi only kicked with her feet in the water.
The executioner pulled her out from the water.
"Our house is ninety-nine *kan* large,[8]
Let's shut her up in a room and seal it

8. *Kan* (or *k'an*) is a unit of measure.

From inside and outside so that she'll die."
So they imprisoned her and forgot about her.
When Aegi was on the brink of death,
A white and a blue crane came down from heaven,
Spread one wing to cushion her, and covered her with another,
And she gave birth to three sons.
She spoke to them:
"If you're truly the sons of the World-Honored One,
Break the lock, go out, and find your maternal grandparents."
They opened the lock with their fingernails
And went out and greeted their grandparents,
Who now realized the boys were their grandsons
And sent them to a local school.
School children tormented them as fatherless.
One day three sons asked their mom to find Dad.
"I slept under the pine tree on the back hill
And conceived you," Mom said.
So they went to the pine tree, bowed, and
Asked it in vain to give them their family name.
They returned and asked their mom again.
"I slept under the juniper and conceived."
The sons went to the juniper and asked the same.
"If you burn incense after your dad's death,
I might become your dad."
The sons returned and told their mom.
"A certain monk spent a night here and I conceived."
The sons asked, "Where can we find our dad?"
Aegi replied: "Climb Heavenly God Mountain, find the abbot,
And ask him to give you your family name."
The sons climbed the mountain and found three roads,
One red, one white, and one blue.
They asked the older which road to take.
He suggested the blue, but the third son objected.
The middle son suggested the red.
The third son objected again and chose the white.
When asked for the reason, he replied,
"To become a Holy One you must walk on the white."
So they trod on and on and, sure enough,
They found Heavenly God Mountain,

Climbed to the temple with ninety-nine monks.
When they entered, the monks talked with the abbot:
"Your sons are here to request the family name."
"What does it mean that the monk has sons?
What on earth are you saying?"
The sons entered and asked for the family name.
The abbot replied, "If you first remove ninety-nine caps
From the monks' heads, mix them, and choose the right one
For each monk, I'll grant you the name."
So the sons did as they were told
And holding the abbot's cap asked,
"Please give us the family name."
"If you go out and enter without leaving footsteps on the sand,
I'll give you your family name."
The sons stepped on the sand and left footprints
But when they returned, a wind smoothed them out.
But the abbot still said he did not know.
"Go down there and bring me a flower
Blossoming on a cliff of folded rocks;
Then I will give you your family name."
The sons went down but could neither scale nor descend.
The three stood on one another's shoulders,
And plucked the flower and brought it.
But the abbot still feigned ignorance.
"Then let's mix our blood and see."
Into a basin filled with water,
Each son bit his finger and dripped blood.
When the abbot did the same,
His drop of blood circled around the sons'.
"Well, nothing can be done now.
I will give you your name.
The first was born at the first watch,
So his name shall be First Watch Son.
The second was born at the second watch,
So his name shall be Second Watch Son.
The third was born at the third watch,
So he shall be Third Watch Son."
After naming them the abbot ascended to heaven.
The sons looked for their Father but lost him again,

So they looked for him where he went,
Riding on a paper horse, and climbed the high heaven.
The abbot looked down and saw them coming.
"No, it won't do!" He threw three fistfuls of shower.
The paper horse got wet and fell.
But the three became living buddhas and flew about.
Just then monks in Korea's eight provinces
Were in search of living buddhas.
They crossed the river and returned with the living buddhas.
The hunter asked what they were carrying.
They answered, "Living buddhas."
The hunter wished to see them:
"If you see them, they will fly away."
But the hunter insisted on seeing them.
So the monks opened the chest,
And the living buddhas flew out
And rested on top of the willow tree.
The monks were unable to retrieve them,
And finally the hunter shot and killed them.
From then on, calamities befell
Korea's hermitages and temples.
O three buddhas, please come to accept our offerings!

P L

Also called "The Seventh Princess" (*Paridegi, Ch'il kongju*), the shamanist narrative song translated here as "The Abandoned Princess" (Princess Pari) is performed at a ritual (known as *chinogi kut*) to pray for the transfer of the soul of the dead to the underworld. Some thirty extant versions can be traced to four regions: central Korea including Seoul, Hamgyŏng (the northeast), the East Sea coast, and Chŏlla (the southwest). The central Korean version emphasizes the princess's heroic acts. In that version her deification is narrated according to the law of cause and effect, and her mythic character can be understood in connection with her attainment of sacred status. In a version transmitted in the Seoul area, she becomes a deity from whom all shamans are descended. In the east coast version she is a deity of the underworld. In the present version she is not a shaman but a princess, and hence does not possess magic power. But because she has revived her dead parents, she becomes a deity who cures illness. In her travels in the underworld, morever, she helps and saves grieving spirits and thus becomes a shamanist deity who takes charge of the underworld, reflecting the human wish to return from death. The princess embodies the virtue of filial piety—even though parents may abandon their child, the child cannot abandon its parents. But her means of reviving her dead parents and recalling the spirits from the underworld are anomalous, for the typical shaman accomplishes it by borrowing the power of a deity.

The version translated here is from Akamatsu Chijō and Akiba Takashi, *Chōsen fuzoku no kenkyū* (Studies in Korean Shamanism; Tokyo: Osakayagō shoten, 1937–1938), narrated by a shaman named Pae Kyŏngjae in Osan, Kyŏnggi province, and annotated by Sŏ Taesŏk and Pak Kyŏngjin, eds., *Sŏsa muga* (Seoul: Koryŏ taehakkyo Minjok munhwa yŏnguso, 1996), pp. 213–253.

The Abandoned Princess

This is a temple the state built with great effort,
And the temple's origin is in the southwest.[9]
Know the heavens!
Above, the indra heaven,[10] blow, the twenty-eight mansions,[11]
The great generals of eight directions, Namong and Muong,[12] all
    have guarded it.
South of the Yangtze lies the Great Han; east of the sea lies
    Chosŏn.[13]
The clan site of the founder of Chosŏn[14] is
Yŏnghŭng, near Tanch'ŏn, in Hamgyŏng province.
Above, on the hundredth memorial day, I lead the living to
    paradise.
Below, on the days of offering,[15] I lead the dead to paradise.
Red mountain wine made of red peonies, white mountain wine
    made of white peonies,
Quietly burning candles, incense fragrance, a cup of wine, and
    wailing,
Today is the day of hope for the spirits.

9. India.

10. The thirty-three heavens, the second of six heavens of form.

11. See Joseph Needham, *Science and Civilization in China* (Cambridge: Cambridge University Press, 1959) 3:239.

12. Eight directional deities. Some identify Namong with the historical monk Naong (d. 1376) and Muong with Muhak (1327–1405).

13. Korea is so called because "it lies east of Parhae" (Pohai). See Peter H. Lee, *Songs of Flying Dragons* (Cambridge: Harvard University Press, 1975), p. 151.

14. Refers to Yi Sŏnggye (1335–1408, r. 1392–1398).

15. Or: the six monthly fast days—on the eight, fourteenth, fifteenth, twenty-third, twenty-ninth, and thirtieth nothing should be eaten after noon.

Kyŏnggi has thirty-seven counties, and Yangju is a large one,[16]
Ch'angdŏk palace, Ch'anghye palace, Kyŏngbok palace,
      Kyŏngdŏk palace,[17]
The lower palace and upper palace, tablets in the royal ancestral
      shrine,
Altars of Soil and Grain—[18]
Our king has succeeded to them all.
Their Majesties the king and queen have put on years,
The audience hall is silent, the queen's chamber empty.
The crown prince is fifteen years old.
"Where are the world's great diviners?
Go and ask our fortune," commands the king.
The ladies-in-waiting reply,
"We have our nameplates, please grant a list of gifts."
What are the gifts?
Five strings of silver coin and five of gold,
Three toe and three hop of pearls,
One *ch'i* and five *p'un*[19] of cloth for the cassock,[20]
Three feet and three inches of silk he bestows.
They go bearing these royal gifts
To shaman Taji of Ch'ŏnha palace, shaman Moran of Chesŏk
      palace,
Shamaness Sosil of Chiha palace, and shaman Kangnim of
      Myŏngdo palace.
They cast pearls and grains of white rice on the white jade tray:
The first sign yields the shaman's fortunes,
The second tells of upper and lower gates,
The third tells the fortune of two majesties.

16. Yangju was an old name for Seoul.

17. All were in Seoul, except for the last, which was in Kaesŏng, built by Yi
Sŏnggye.

18. An altar "symbolizes the land and its contribution to life, which served as
important national altars." The ruler offered sacrifices there in spring and autumn.
Charles O. Hucker, *A Dictionary of Official Titles in Imperial China* (Stanford:
Stanford University Press, 1985), p. 416b. For more on the altars of soil and grain
see my *Songs of Flying Dragons*, pp. 125–128.

19. One *toe* makes ten *hop*; *ch'i* is the Korean inch, one-tenth of a *cha*, and *p'un*
is one-tenth of an inch.

20. In the original *kasawi*, whose meaning is unclear. I follow Sŏ Taesŏk's
reading.

"I fear to tell you but cannot deceive you.
If you hold a marriage ceremony in an unlucky year,
You'll have seven princesses.
If in a lucky year, three princes."
Thus they inform the king.
"One moment is long as three autumns, one day as ten.
How can we await an auspicious year?"
The king calls all his officials
And orders the office of astrologer to choose a day.
On the third day of the third month is the first selection;
On the fifth day of the fifth month, the second selection;
On the seventh day of the seventh month
When the Herdboy and Weaver[21] meet
On the bridge built by crows and magpies,
The chief of royal weddings makes the third selection.
Three thousand troops on the low road,
Five thousand on the high road,[22]
Cavalry in rows of five guard the royal carriage.
Courtiers in black belt prepare the bridal room in a separate
    palace.
The geese are presented on the jade table,[23] the nuptial cups
    exchanged.
All the officials cry, "Long live the king!"
His Majesty returns to T'ongmyŏng Hall,
And the queen[24] to the inner palace.
And the people cry, "Long live the king!"
Time flows like a river, heartless time flows like a stream.
In a gust of wind three summer months have passed,
And strange symptoms appear in the queen[25]

21. Herdboy (or Draught Ox) and Weaver: constellations in Chinese astronomy, on both sides of the Milky Way; often invoked as a fit metaphor for the separation of lovers. Fated to a year-long separation, they meet once on the night of the seventh day of the seventh lunar month, when magpies form a bridge across the river of stars.

22. This may allude to the boundary between this world and the other world.

23. At the marriage rite, the groom presents a pair of wooden geese as a symbol of conjugal love.

24. Here her name is given as Ch'iltae; in another version it is Kiltae.

25. The lines describe symptoms of pregnancy.

The royal rice tastes raw,
The royal water tastes foul,
Golden glow tobacco tastes like grass,[26]
The royal soup tastes like soy sauce.
"Present the fruits of five hundred bearing trees
Brought through the four great gates to the inner palace."
Among mandarin duck adorned quilts and pillows,[27]
A breeze at the east window cannot reach the west window.[28]
When ladies-in-waiting inform His Majesty, he orders,
"Consult the shaman of Ch'ŏnha palace!"
Shaman Taji of Ch'ŏnha palace, shaman Moran of Chesŏk
    palace,
They cast coral beads on the jade tray.
The first sign yields the shaman's fortune,
The second tells of upper and lower gates,
The third yields the royal fortune:
"When it comes to pass Your Majesty will know—
Had you married next year, a year of auspice,
A prince would've been born to rule with two brothers.
But you married in an unlucky year, so you will have the first
    princess."
Ladies-in-waiting report these words to both Their Majesties.
"What do they know?" they retort.
One, two months pass; in the third the fetus forms.
Small bones seem to melt, big bones squeezed.[29]
Five and a half months pass;
"Midwives of the inner and outer chambers,
Royal messengers and servants,
All the officials and three thousand court ladies
Inquire at the inner palace morning, noon, and night."
After seven months, after nine months,
Black silk supports before, blue silk supports behind,[30]

26. The name of a tobacco produced in Kwangju, Kyŏnggi.

27. *Chatpyŏgae:* a pillow made of chestnut wood, or simply embroidered pillow.

28. She finds her daily routine difficult, she finds it hard to move about, referring to her state of "physiological crisis."

29. The soreness of the pregnant woman is described here. Folk belief has it that the material of the baby's bones is drawn from the mother's bones.

30. A support (bolster, pillow) to elevate her body or cushion her for comfort.

"Present all fabrics entering the four great gates to the inner
    palace!"
Prisoners are released in every town, the royal academy closed,
Ten months have passed, the delivery room is ready.
After an easy labor and birth,
The queen turns around—a princess is born.
Ladies-in-waiting and three thousand court ladies
Announce to His Majesty the princess's birth.
His Majesty commands:
"Inquire of the queen her dreams."
The queen replies, "I dreamed of this one day:
From one shoulder rose the moon,
And from the other rose the sun."
The king commands:
"To hold and carry, walk and nurse the baby,
The court lady for the royal son-in-law and supervision.
Blue silk supports before, black silk supports behind,
Among silk screens in the inner room,
Raise this baby with utmost care."
"May we humbly ask you to name this child?"
"Her name is Princess Pink Peach, another name Moon Girl."
Oh and alas! One soul among the dead,
Upon the first princess's birth
Released from three years' mourning, consoling the spirits in the
    underworld,
From ancestors' cause of grievance,
From the karma of earthly existence,
The dead man sheds his head cover, the dead woman her *yomo*
    cap,[31]
With prayers for rebirth in the Land of Happiness,
Becomes a man and journeys to Amitābha's Pure Land,
Upon this very day.

Time flows like river, the princess is three years old.
Strange symptoms appear in the queen.
Among mandarin duck embroidered quilts and pillows,
A breeze at the east window cannot reach the west window.

31. This might refer to the hollowed (indented) woman's cap.

Small bones seem to melt, big bones squeezed.
The royal rice tastes raw,
The royal water tastes foul,
Golden glow tobacco tastes like grass,
The royal soup tastes like soy sauce.
"Present the fruits of five hundred bearing trees
Brought through the four great gates to the inner palace."
In three months, the fetus forms;
Five and a half months pass;
After seven months, after nine months,
The delivery room and six physicians are ready.
"Ladies-in-waiting and eunuchs
Attend the queen morning, noon, and night."
In the tenth month, pearl-sewn recliner cast aside,
Labor and birth over, the queen turns around to view the baby:
The second princess is born.
"I've given birth to girls. Surely I'll have a boy soon."
"To hold and carry, walk and nurse this baby,
The court lady for the royal son-in-law and supervision.
Black silk supports before, blue silk supports behind,
Among silk screens in the inner room,
Raise this baby with utmost care."
Oh and alas! One soul among the dead,
Upon the second princess's birth,
Pushes open the gates of Knife Mountain Hell,
The gates of Eighty-Four Thousand Hells, and
Journeys to Amitābha's Pure Land, the Land of Happiness.

Time flows like a dream,
The second princess is three years old.
Strange symptoms appear again in the queen.
Among mandarin duck embroidered quilts and pillows,
A breeze at the east window cannot reach the west window.
Small bones seem to melt, big bones squeezed.
The royal rice tastes raw,
The royal water tastes foul,
Golden glow tobacco tastes like grass,
The royal soup tastes like soy sauce.
"Present the fruits of five hundred bearing trees

Brought through the four great gates to the inner palace."
In three months, the fetus forms;
Five and a half months pass;
After seven months, after nine months,
The delivery room and six physicians are ready.
"Ladies-in-waiting and eunuchs
Attend the queen morning, noon, and night."
In the tenth month, pearl-sewn recliner cast aside,
Labor and birth over, the queen turns around to view the baby:
The third princess is born.
"I've given birth to girls. Surely I'll have a boy soon."
"To hold and carry, walk and nurse the baby,
The court lady for the royal son-in-law and supervision.
Blue silk supports before, black silk supports behind,
Among silk screens in the inner room,
Raise this baby with utmost care."
Oh and alas! One soul among the dead,
Upon the third princess's birth,
Pushes open the gates of Knife Mountain Hell,
The gates of Eighty-Four Thousand Hells, and
Journeys to Amitābha's Pure Land, the Land of Happiness.

Time flows like a dream,
The third princess is three years old.
Strange symptoms appear in the queen.
Among mandarin duck embroidered quilts and pillows,
A breeze at the east window cannot reach the west window.
Small bones seem to melt, big bones squeezed.
The royal rice tastes raw,
The royal water tastes foul,
Golden glow tobacco tastes like grass,
The royal soup tastes like soy sauce.
"Present the fruits of five hundred bearing trees
Brought through the four great gates to the inner palace."
The ladies-in-waiting inform His Majesty.
"Consult the diviner of Ch'ŏnha palace."
"Please, bestow the gifts," they ask.
He sends five strings of silver coin, five of gold,
Three toe and three hop of pearls,

One foot and one inch of cloth for the cassock,
Three feet and three inches of silk he bestows.
They go bearing these royal gifts
To shaman Taji of Ch'ŏnha palace, shamaness Sosil of Chiha
    palace,
Shaman Kangnim of Myŏngdo palace, and shaman Moran of
    Chesŏk palace.
They cast pearls and grains of white rice on the white jade tray:
The first yields the shaman's fortune,
The second tells of upper and lower gates,
The third tells the royal fortune.
"I fear to tell you but cannot deceive you.
You should have married in a year of auspice;
Since you married in an unlucky year,
The fourth princess will be born."
Ladies-in-waiting report these words to both Their Majesties:
"What do they know?" they retort.
One and two months pass, and in three months
The fetus forms;
Five and a half months pass;
"Midwives of inner and outer chambers,
Royal messengers and servants,
All the officials and three thousand court ladies
Inquire at the inner palace morning, noon, and night."
After seven months, after nine full months,
Blue silk supports before, black silk supports behind,
"Present all cloths entering the four great gates to the inner
    palace."
Ten months have passed, the delivery room is ready,
Labor and birth over, the queen turns around to view the baby:
The fourth princess is born.
"I've given birth to girls. Surely I'll have a boy soon."
"To hold and carry, walk and nurse the baby,
The court lady for the royal son-in-law and supervision.
Black silk supports before, blue silk supports behind,
Among silk screens in the inner room,
Raise this baby too with utmost care."
Oh and alas! One among the dead,
Upon this princess's birth

Released from three years' mourning, consoling the spirits in the
    underworld,
From ancestors' cause of grievance,
From the karma of earthly existence,
The dead man sheds his head cover, the dead woman her yomo
    cap,
With prayers for rebirth in the Land of Happiness,
Becomes a man and journeys to Amitābha's Pure Land,
Upon this very day.

Heartless time flows like a stream, like a dream,
The fourth princess is three years old.
Strange symptoms appear in the queen.
Among mandarin duck embroidered quilts and pillows,
A breeze at the east window cannot reach the west window.
Small bones seem to melt, big bones squeezed.
The royal rice tastes raw,
The royal water tastes foul,
Golden glow tobacco tastes like grass,
The royal soup tastes like soy sauce.
"Present the fruits of five hundred bearing trees
Brought through the four great gates to the inner palace."
In three months, the fetus forms;
Five and a half months pass.
After seven months, after nine months,
She rejects the pearl-sewn bolster.
Ten months pass, and after labor and birth,
The queen turns around to view the baby:
Another princess is born.
"I've given birth to girls. Surely I'll have a boy soon."
"To hold and carry, walk and nurse the baby,
The court lady for the royal son-in-law and supervision.
Blue silk supports before, black silk supports behind,
Among silk screens in the inner room,
Raise this baby with utmost care."
Oh and alas! One among the dead,
Upon the birth of the fifth princess,
Released from three years' mourning,
consoling the spirits in the underworld,

From ancestors' cause of grievance,
From the karma of earthly existence,
The dead man sheds his head cover, the dead woman her yomo
    cap,
With prayers for rebirth in the Land of Happiness,
Becomes a man and journeys to Amitābha's Pure Land,
Upon this very day.

Time flows like a river, the princess is three years old.
Strange symptoms appear in the queen.
Among mandarin duck embroidered quilts and pillows,
A breeze at the east window cannot reach the west window.
The ladies-in-waiting inform His Majesty.
"Consult the diviner of Ch'ŏnha palace!"
"Please, bestow the gifts," they ask.
Five strings of silver coin, five of gold,
Three toe and three hop of pearls,
Three feet and three inches of silk,
And one ch'i and one p'un of cloth for the cassock.
They go bearing these royal gifts
To shaman Taji of Ch'ŏnha palace, shamaness Sosil of Chiha
    palace,
Shaman Moran of Chesŏk palace, shaman Kangnim of Myŏngdo
    palace.
They cast pearls and grains of white rice on the white jade tray:
The first throw yields the shaman's fortune,
The second tells of upper and lower gates,
The third tells the fortune of two majesties.
"Her Majesty is indeed with child;
But since you married in an unlucky year,
The sixth princess will be born."
"What do they know?" they retort.
One and two months pass, the fetus forms in the third,
Five and a half months pass;
"Midwives of inner and outer chambers,
Royal messengers and servants,
All the officials and three thousand court ladies
Inquire at the inner palace morning, noon, and night."
After seven months, after nine full months,

Blue silk supports before, black silk supports behind,
"Present all cloths entering the four great gates to the inner
    palace."
Ten months have passed, the delivery room is ready,
Labor and birth over, the queen turns around to view the baby:
Another princess is born.
"I've given birth to girls. Surely I'll have a boy soon."
"To hold and carry, walk and nurse the baby,
The court lady for the royal son-in-law and supervision.
Among silk screens in the inner room,
Raise this baby too with utmost care."
Oh and alas! One among the dead,
Upon the sixth princess's birth
Released from three years' mourning, consoling the spirits in the
    underworld,
From ancestors' cause of grievance,
From the karma of earthly existence,
The dead man sheds his head cover, the dead woman her yomo cap,
With prayers for rebirth in the Land of Happiness,
Becomes a man and journeys to Amitābha's Pure Land,
Upon this very day.

The country of a thousand tricents of mountains and rivers,
Time flows by like a dream.
All six princesses are invested.
The queen again has strange symptoms.
Among mandarin duck embroidered quilts and pillows,
A breeze at the east window cannot reach the west window.
Small bones seem to melt, big bones squeezed.
The royal rice tastes raw,
The royal water tastes foul,
Golden glow tobacco tastes like grass,
The royal soup tastes like soy sauce.
"Present the fruits of five hundred bearing trees
Brought through the four great gates to the inner palace!"
Her face, once fair as lotus,
Is now gaunt, pitiful to view.
With her delicate body how can she endure?
His Majesty asks, "What are your dreams?"

"I saw perched on my right hand a purple falcon,
And on my left hand a white falcon.
I saw a golden turtle resting on my knees,
And the sun and moon rising from my shoulders.
On the main beam of Great Bright Hall,
I saw entwined blue and gold dragons."
This time the dream portends a prince.
"Ladies-in-waiting, consult the shaman of Ch'ŏnha palace."
"Please, bestow the gifts," they ask.
Five strings of silver coin, five of gold,
Three toe and three hop of pearls,
One ch'i and one p'un of cloth for the cassock,
Three feet and three inches of silk he bestows.
They go bearing these royal gifts
To shaman Taji of Ch'ŏnha palace, shamaness Sosil of Chiha
    palace,
Shaman Moran of Chesŏk palace, and shaman Kangnim of
    Myŏngdo palace.
They cast pearls and grains of white rice on the white jade tray:
The first throw yields the shaman's fortune;
The second tells of upper and lower gates;
The third tells the fortune of two majesties.
"You will find out later,
It is clear that the queen is with child,
But since you married in an unlucky year,
She will give birth to a seventh princess."
So they report to His Majesty.
"However well they divine, what do they know?"
As her dreams foretold,
In the third month the fetus forms.
Five and a half months pass, seven months pass,
Inner and outer delivery rooms and six physicians stand ready.
"Royal messengers and servants
Inquire after the queen morning, noon, and night."
Proclaim in the five wards, notify eight provinces,
Post it on the four great gates; he approves
That the prison gates be open and prisoners set free.
After the eighth month, after the ninth month,
Now it's the tenth month, and she rejects the pearl-sewn bolster.

Labor and birth over, she turns around to view the baby:
It's the seventh princess.
Her Majesty the queen weeps royal tears.
His Majesty inquires: "Ladies-in-waiting,
In the deep deep deepest recess of the palace
Why is that sound of a woman wailing?"
The ladies-in-waiting reply,
"We fear to tell you but cannot deceive you . . . "
"Ladies-in-waiting, you too are brazen!
How can you face me?"
He strikes the desk with royal hand:
"What sins of my former lives were so great
Heaven has given me seven daughters?"
He scatters his incense box and stands:
"Who'll worship at the altars of soil and grain?
Who will inherit the state and throne?
Who will inherit the country and people?"
His Majesty commands:
"Ladies-in-waiting, three thousand court ladies,
Take that baby and cast her in the rear garden!"
Her Majesty replies:
"They say the state law ignores blood ties
In the interests of the country,
But how can you cast her out?
One among courtiers and ladies-in-waiting,
Take her as foster-child."
"The state laws are not so,
There's nothing we can do."
Dressed in the seventh-day culottes and trousers,
A slip inscribed with the time of birth
Tied to her coat strings,
The baby is cast away in the rear garden.
Mountains are deep and waters still.
A sudden gale arises.
Unexpectedly, crows and magpies descend
And cushion her with one wing, cover her with the other.

It is a warm spring day.
With the royal guard and steward, His Majesty

Goes to view blossoms and willows in the rear garden.
To the east he sees a wondrous light in the air
And hears crows and magpies crying loudly.
"A wondrous light in the air bodes well.
What's over there that makes crows and magpies cry noisily?"
Ladies-in-waiting reply:
"You told us to abandon the baby born this time.
We dared not defy your order,
So we cast her away in the rear garden.
One can still hear her cries faintly."
Her Majesty the queen commands:
"Carry the baby and bring her here."
Behold, black ants fill her ears,
Golden ants her mouth,
Small ants her eyes.
On Her Majesty's lotus face she let
Pearl-like tears flow two by two.
"They say the state law ignores blood ties
In the interests of the country.
But why cast her out so heartlessly?"
His Majesty commands: "Courtiers, I shall send her as an
      offering
To the Dragon Kings of the four seas to atone for my sins.
Let a box maker make a fine jade box."
The queen lays the baby within it,
At its mouth a jade bottle with milk from her breasts,
And ties to her coat strings a slip
Inscribed with the month and hour of birth.
Her Majesty then pleads:
"How can you cast your own child into the sea?
Let some childless minister adopt her; or,
If she must be abandoned, at least give her a name."
"Paridŏgi, the throwaway, Tŏjidŏgi, the castaway."
Loosely she closes the jade box with the golden turtle lock
And engraves in golden letters: "The Seventh Princess."
The Minister of Rites is called in.
He receives three cups of royal wine and takes the box on his
      back.
He leaves the palace gate but does not know where to go.

Then crows and magpies bow their heads to lead him,
And grasses and trees bend down.
One thousand tricents, two thousand tricents,
Three thousand tricents they go.
Kalch'i Mount and Kalchi'i Pass, Pulch'i Mount and Pulch'i
    Pass.[32]
Heave-ho heave-ho,[33] he goes, calling the name of Amitābha.
He crosses the pass and then moves on,
Before them the River of Yellow Springs,
Behind, the River of Flowing Sands.
He casts her in the magpie shoals in the sea of blood.
First the foams rise; then pillars of waves surge high;
Third, the waters turn blood-red.
Thunder and lightning quake.
Suddenly a golden turtle appears and bearing the box upon its
    back
Swims off somewhere into the Eastern Sea.
Crows and magpies gather to cushion her with one wing
And cover her with the other.
At night, clouds and fog lay thick,
Daytime clouds and fog lay thick.
World-Honored Śākyamuni is touring the four seas
With the honored Maudgalyāyana and Kāśyapa[34]
And has come to bestow babies on human beings.
"What is it over there,
What makes the crows and magpies cry so long
And a wondrous light shine in the air?
If human, it is one favored by heaven,
If beast, it is one favored by heaven,
If spirit, it is one favored by heaven.
Go and see what it is."
"Lacking the virtue, we can see nothing."

32. Imaginary places.

33. *Ŏsadi taesadi* give a hard push or pull; the difficulty of climbing seems to be implied.

34. Maudgalyāyana: one of the ten chief disciples of śākyamuni, noted for miraculous power; for a story of how he rescues his mother from the underworld, see Victor H. Mair, *Traditional Chinese Literature*, pp. 1093–1127. Kāśyapa: after Śākyamuni's extinction Kāśyapa became leader of his disciples.

Then holding the *Yellow Scripture*[35] in his hand,
Śākyamuni looks at west village over the great ocean
As they row their stone boat speedily.
A jade box is left there!
"If this were a boy I would make him my disciple;
But being a girl she is no use to me."
He hides the box in the hollow of a hazel tree.
Hemp skullcap pulled down,
Purple packs upon their backs,
Singing the songs of hell,
An old man and woman who pray for merits[36] pass by.
World-Honored Śākyamuni asks:
"Are you human or are you ghost?"
"We are not ghosts, nor beasts.
We're old man and woman praying for merit
And guarding this mountain."
World-Honored Śākyamuni speaks:
"Tell me, what is merit?
Build a bridge over deep waters to help the traveler,
Build a monastery to save mankind. Clothe the naked,
Feed the hungry, give water to the thirsty.
But to nourish the baby who has no mother's milk
Is the greatest merit of all.
How about taking this child and raising it?"
The old man and woman reply:
"In spring, summer, and fall we live in the fields,
In winter we stay in a cave."
"If you keep and raise this child,
You will have food to eat and clothes to wear,
And a small thatched cottage will appear."
In an instant, Śākyamuni is gone.
Clearly it is the Buddha's power.
They hear the baby's cries
Among green willows and yellow cuckoo,
Between the willows where yellow birds fly.
They find a jade box where the sounds come,

35. Perhaps referring to the *Scripture of the Yellow Court.*
36. Or old beggar man and old beggar woman.

Examine it to find that the golden turtle lock is ajar.
Aejung Scripture for the parents,
Loyalty Scripture for the country,
Love Scripture for the wife and children,
And *Ch'ŏnji P'aryang Scripture*,[37]
They chant them all one by one,
And without a key the jade box opens.
They look inside: red ants fill her eyes,
Worms and snakes coil around her waist.
They wash her from bottom to top
In the current of Long Flowing Stream,
Shed their long-sleeved cassock and wash her twice more,
Taking off their long-sleeved fin garments,
And when they carry her and turn around,
A small cottage exquisitely stands there.

Eight, nine years go by.
Untaught, she is versed in the science of the heavens and the
    earth
As well as all the secret military arts.
One day she asks, "Grandma, Grandpa,
Even flying birds and crawling insects have their own parents.
Where is my own mom, where is my own dad?
Find me my parents, please."
"Grandpa is your dad and Grandma your mom."
"Grandma and Grandpa, please don't lie.
How can such old people have a child like me?"
Being childless and lonely, they hoped to rely on her.
"Heaven is your dad, and earth your mom."
"Heaven and earth give birth to myriad things,
But how can they give birth to a human being?
Grandma and grandpa, please tell me the truth."
"You cut a bamboo stalk in Chŏlla province,
Cut both ends to make a staff and hold it[38]
Through three years' mourning for a dead father.

37. All imaginary texts.
38. The chief mourner carries a bamboo staff in a man's funeral, and a paulownia staff in a woman's.

Chŏlla bamboo is your dad, and
Your mom is the paulownia on the back hill."
"The Chŏlla bamboo is far, far away,
I cannot inquire after it three times a day."
So the child daily sends regards
To the paulownia tree on the back hill.

Time flows like a river, and the girl is now fifteen.
One day they see in the child's washbasin
The sun and moon fallen there.
Thus time flows on like a river.
Their Majesties are gravely ill.
The king commands, "Go consult the shaman of Ch'ŏnha
     palace."
"Please bestow the gifts."
He sends five strings of silver coin and five of gold,
One ch'i and one p'un of cloth for the cassock,
Three toe and three hop of pearls,
Three feet and three inches of silk—
They go bearing these royal gifts
To shaman Taji of Ch'ŏnha palace,
And shaman Moran of Chesŏk palace.
They cast pearls and grains of white rice on the white jade tray:
The first throw yields the shaman's fortune,
The second tells of upper and lower gates,
The third the fortune of two majesties.
"When it comes to pass Your Majesty will see
As surely as the sun sets in the West Sea
And the moon rises from the East Sea.
Your Majesties will die on the same day and hour.
Go find the seventh princess where you abandoned her."
Thus they report to the king and queen.
"If only we had left her on level ground,
Our ministers could find her.
But who can find her now?"
Both Majesties dream on the same day and time:
Six azure-clad boys descend from the beam of Great Bright Hall
And bow before them. Their Majesties ask,
"Are you human or are you ghosts?

Even flying birds cannot enter here;
Why did you come in?"
"We are not human beings nor ghosts.
We're the azure-clad boys of heaven,
Who came at the Jade Emperor's bidding
To take Your Majesty's life tablet
To store it in the city of dead."
"But why is it so?
Did some ministers send a message of grievance?
Or the people complain about me?"
"Neither the people's complaint nor the minister's grievance.
You sinned when you cast out the child sent by heaven,
So you will take ill and die
On the same day and at the same hour."
"But how can we be saved?"
"Seek the child and take her back.
When you seek the elixir of Three Blessed Mounts,
The sacred water of Peerless Transcendent,
The magic pearl of the Dragon King of the Eastern Sea,
The kayam plant of Mount Pongnae,
And the suru plant of Ana Mountain.[39]
When you eat of these you'll be saved."
Suddenly they awake; it was an empty dream.
At dawn the king summons his ministers:
"If one of you finds the abandoned child,
We'll reward him a thousand gold coins
And enfeoffment of myriad households.
Indeed, I shall grant him half the kingdom."
The ministers are silent.
"He who brings only the sacred water
Will be lord of myriad households."
"The Eastern Sea Dragon palace is a heavenly place,
The Western Sea Dragon palace is also a heavenly place.
Though we die we cannot go there.
We would gladly look for her on flat land,
But who can find an abandoned child among the waters?"
Then the Minister of Rites speaks:

39. *Kayam* (the hazel tree) and *suruch'wi*: herbs that confer immortality.

"For many generations my house has served the throne,
How can I sit idly now?
I shall find the princess, even if I perish on the way."
"What would you like to take with you?"
Bearing letters from the king, queen, and six princesses
And the small clothes of the seventh princess,
Escorted by palace ladies two by two,
They leave through the five garrison gates and palace gate,
But they do not know where to go.
Then crows and magpies bow their heads to guide them,
And grasses and trees bend down to lead them.
A country of a thousand tricents of mountains and rivers,
Mountains rise fold upon fold,
The cuckoo cries sadly.
Golden warblers flit among the willows,
Before the River of Yellow Springs,
Behind the River of Flowing Sands.
Kalch'i Mount and Kalch'i Pass,
Pulch'i Mount and Pulch'i Pass.
Invoking the name of Amitābha,
At last they come to Taesang Cloister.
An old man and woman praying for merit ask:
"Are you human or are you ghosts?
How have you come where
Flying birds and crawling insects cannot enter?"
"I've come to take you upon the king's orders."
"If I am indeed the daughter of a king,
Great were my sins to have been cast out the moment I was
    born."
"I bring the jacket you wore as a seven-day baby."
"How am I to recognize it?"
"I bring the record of the month and hour of your birth."
"How am I to remember it?"
"I bring letters from the king, queen, and six princesses."
"What do their letters mean to me? Bring me a sign!"
He has a golden vessel with drops of blood
From the thumbs of the king and queen.
He pricks the child's fourth finger:
The bloods blend and blossom like a cloud.

Now the girl agrees to go.
"Shall we await your command with the royal guards?
Shall we await your command with the princess's palanquin?"
"I who was cast out at birth,
What use have I for a palanquin?
Give me a horse, I shall ride alone."
She follows the Minister of Rites and presents herself at the
    palace gate.
The king and queen command: "Let the princess come in
    quickly."
They grasp each other's hands and shed royal tears.
"Did we abandon you in hatred? No, it was in anger.
We cast you out in anger. How did you bear the cold?
How did you bear the heat?
How did you bear the hunger?
How did you bear the longing for your parents?"
"I lived by the merit of an old man and woman."

A country of a thousand tricents of mountains and rivers,
Cruel time rushes past.
The illness of Their Majesties is grave.
"All the officials, ladies-in-waiting, and people—
Will you fetch the sacred water of Peerless Transcendent to save
    the country?"
"That is not a medicine of this world.
How can we obtain it?"
They call the eldest princess: "Will you go to save your parents?"
"How can I go where three thousand court ladies cannot go?"
They call the second princess: "Will you go to save your
    parents?"
"How can I go where my elder sister cannot go?"
They call the third princess: "Will you go to save your parents?"
"How can I go where my two elder sisters cannot go?"
They call the fourth princess: "Will you go to save your
    parents?"
"How can I go where my three elder sisters cannot go?"
They call the fifth princess: "Will you go to save your parents?"
"How can I go where my four sisters cannot?"
They call the sixth princess: "Will you go to save your parents?"

"How can I go where my five elder sisters cannot?"
They call the seventh princess: "Will you go to save your
     parents?"
"I have no debt to this country.
But I'm grateful to my mother who bore me for ten months.
I shall go for my mother's sake."
"Would you have the royal guards or the princess's palanquin?"
"I shall ride alone," she says.
She wears a coarse top and bottom and outer coat,
Binds her hair in double knots,
With a bamboo hat and an iron staff,
And a silver backpack with golden straps.
She receives the signatures of the king and queen and binds them
     to her belt,
She receives the signatures of six princesses and binds them to
     her belt.
"Six elder sisters, three thousand court ladies,
Even if Their Majesties die on the same day and same hour,
Do not perform a funeral but await my return."
She bids farewell to the king, queen, and six princesses
And gallops out the palace gate but doesn't know where to go.
Oh and alas, one among the dead,
If it follows the seventh princess,
With prayer for rebirth in the Pure Land of the West,
Then it becomes a man and enters the Land of Happiness
Upon this very day.

She brandishes her staff once and goes a thousand tricents,
She brandishes it twice and two thousand tricents,
She brandishes it thrice and three thousand tricents.
What is the season now? It is the third month of spring, a
     pleasant time.
Plum and peach are in bloom,
Fragrant flowers and grasses wave gently.
Yellow warblers fly among the willows,
Parrots and peacocks preen, the cuckoo calls its mate.
The sun sets over the western mountain,
And the moon rises from the eastern peak.
She sits and scans far-off a golden rock

Covered with low pines with even branches.
There Śākyamuni explains the dharma
To bodhisattva Kṣītigarbha[40] and Buddha Amitābha,
She draws near and bows thrice three times.
"Are you a human being or ghost?"
Here where flying birds and crawling insects cannot enter,
How did you come?"
"I am His Majesty's heir apparent on a mission of filial service.
Now I have lost my way.
Please, guide me by your grace."
World-Honored Śākyamuni replies:
"I have heard that the king has seven girls,
But this is the first I've heard of an heir apparent.
When they cast you out at the west village of the Great Sea,
I saved your wretched life.
But that was then.
You traversed three thousand tricents on level earth,
But how can you go three thousand tricents of steep path?"
"Though I die on the way, I will go."
"Take this gift of a udumbara flower.[41]
When you come to a great sea, wave this flower
And the sea will become hard ground."
Before her she sees walls of thorns and iron, reaching to the sky.
She remembers the Buddha's words and waves the flower:
Armless demons, legless demons, eyeless demons,
A hundred million demons jump and croak like frogs,
Open the gates of Hell of Knife Mountain
And Hell of Fire Mountain,
The eight thousand four hundred hells.
Souls headed for ten kings of hell are sent there,
Souls destined for the hell are sent there.
Oh and alas! One soul among the dead,
With rotten ears and rotten mouth,

40. Kṣītigarbha: a bodhisattva who vowed to save all people from the world. He enters hell to save the wicked.

41. In the original, *nahwa* (gauze flower), referring to the *udumbara*, ficus glomerata, that symbolizes the appearance of a Buddha in the world. It is said to blossom only once in every three thousand years.

If it hears prayers and repeats them to all the bodhisattvas,
It follows Princess Pari and enters
The Pure Land of the West, the Land of Happiness,
On this very day.

She views a place afar—
To the east a gate of blue glass,
To the west a gate of white glass,
To the south a gate of red glass,
To the north a gate of black glass,
And in the center the gate of chastity,
And there stands the Peerless Transcendent.
His height seems to reach the sky,
Face like a rice cake, eyes like an oil cup for a lamp,
Nose like a clay bottle, hands large as kettle lids,
Feet three feet and three inches long,
So dreadful and frightful he is.
She backs away and bows three times.
Peerless Transcendent asks:
"Are you a human being or ghost that you enter here
Where flying birds and crawling insects cannot?
How did you enter and where do you come from?"
"I am an heir apparent on a mission of filial service."
"If you came to fetch the water, what payment do you bring?
And for the herbs what payment do you bring?"
"In my haste I forgot to bring anything."
"Then draw the water for three years,
Tend the fire for three years,
Gather the herbs for three years."
After thrice three years of life here,
The Peerless Transcendent speaks to her:
"You seem a prince behind, but a woman before.
Why not tie a marriage bond,
Bear me seven sons and then return? How about that?"
"If that's for my parents' sake, I'll do it."
Heaven and earth for canopy, creepers for a pillow,
Grass for bed, a cloud bank for shade,
The morning star for lamp.
In the first watch she gives her consent,

In the second watch she stays,
And throughout the night they tie the marriage knot.

She bears seven sons, and one day she speaks,
"However great our love may be,
I have delayed my mission for my parents.
I dreamed in the first watch a silver bowl was shattered
And in the second a silver spoon broken.
Surely the king and queen must have died at the same time.
I must hurry now to save them."
"Take it in your golden crock,
The water you drew is healing water.
Take the herbs you gathered
For they bring flesh and bone to life.
But first, won't you view the sea with me?"
"I don't care to view the sea."
"Then come view the back hill's flowers."
"I don't care to see the flowers."
"I lived alone as a bachelor,
But now, how can eight bachelors live?
Please, take seven boys with you."
"I'll do that for my parents' sake."
Big children walk and small ones are carried on backs.
Then the Peerless Transcendent asks her,
"What if I were to follow you?"
"It is said that wife should follow husband;
For my parents' sake let it be so.
I came alone, now nine bodies return."

Before the River of Yellow Springs,
Behind the River of Flowing Sands.
Princess Pari asks, "What are those boats row on row
Over the Magpie Shoal in the Sea of Blood?"
"Those carry souls that in the former life
Were filial to parents, loyal to the state,
Loved their brothers, and kept harmony in their homes."
Oh and alas! One among the dead goes forth,
At the first shrine receives the ritual coins,
At the second the preliminary purification ritual

At the third feed to three messengers of the underworld,[42]
The iron gate, the bamboo gate, lotus hall,
The forty-ninth day ritual to the soul of the dead.
He receives gold and silver coins,
Invokes the name of the Buddha, and
Rides the boat to the Pure Land of the West, the Land of
    Happiness.
She asks, "Those bottomless boats upon the Sea of Blood,
Crying like summer frogs as they go,
What boats are they?"
"Those carry souls who in the former life were unfilial,
Betrayed the state, didn't love their brothers,
Gave with small measure and took with large measure,
Gave bad rice for alms and harmed others.
Now those boats carry their souls crying
To the hundred million four thousand hells."
"And what are those boats without rowers?"
"Those are the boats of souls
Who in the former life had no offspring,
And now drift on the sea."
"Herdboys on Mount Ch'o,
In the capital's broad square over there,
Why are the people gathered?"
"We'll tell you if you pay a toll."
"And what's the toll?"
She gives them seven feet and seven inches of silk
That strapped the baby to her back.
Then the herdboy speaks:
"Unborn babies may not know it,
But those come forth from the womb know
That the king and queen died on the same day
And today is the state funeral.
Are you a human being or ghost?
The seventh princess has gone three thousand tricents to seek
    the sacred water,

42. *Saje samsŏng* in the original, for which see Cho Hŭngyun, *Hanguk ŭi shamŏnijŭm* (Korean shamanism) (Seoul: Seoul taehakkyo ch'ulp'anbu, 1999), pp. 163–166.

But there is no news whether she is alive or dead."
Startled, the seventh princess hastens.
Hiding seven sons in a thicket
And the Peerless Transcendent in the forest,
She stares at the funeral flags—indeed, they're the king's,
She sees the dragon robe and dirge—they're the king's.
Loosening their hair, they announce death.
"Ladies-in-waiting, attend within the curtains,
People and ministers, guard outside the curtains,
Lower the small bier, lower the large bier."
She raises the coffin lid and drives the people back,
Loosens the seven knots that bind each corpse,
Infuses breath into their flesh,
Infuses breath into their bones,
Inserts magic pearls into their eyes,
Pours sacred water into their mouths,
And they revive at the same time.
The king arises, "I've slept deep.
Have we come out to view the sea
Or to view flowers on the back hill?"
"Not to view the sea, nor the flowers;
Your Majesties died, and we're in the funeral procession.
The seventh princess went three thousand tricents
To the Weakwater to obtain the sacred water,[43]
And you have revived on this day and hour."
His Majesty cancels the funeral, declares it an outing,
And returns to T'ongmyŏng Hall,
And the queen to the inner palace.
The officials and three thousand court ladies all shout,
"Long live the king!"
Myriad people cry in unison, "Long live the king!"
His Majesty summons the seventh princess:
"All my officials and ministers have inquired after us,
Why has the seventh princess not come?"

43. The name of a transcendent stream on which not even a feather can float.
See Joseph Needham, *Science and Civilization in China* (Cambridge: Cambridge
University Press, 1959) 3:608–611.

"She has sinned, she married the Peerless Transcendent
And bore him seven sons."
"The sin is not yours but mine.
Should I give you half of my kingdom?
Or all fabric brought through the four great gates?"
"Had I once held the kingdom, I'd now desire it.
Had I once had the clothes, I'd want them.
But I never knew fine food and clothes at my parents' knee,
So I will become the progenitor of shamans."

Above on the hundredth day, she leads the living to paradise,
Below on the six fast days she leads the dead to paradise.
Above, embroidered jacket made from Chinese silk,
Below, a long skirt, embroidered shoes, and a staff,
A bell at her hand, broad red sash at her waist,
A fifty-ribbed fan in one hand,[44]
She governs all shamans.[45]

"Present the Peerless Transcendent, my son-in-law," the king
     commands.
"His gauze cap will catch upon the south gate."
"Dig out the soil beneath the gate and enter."
"His waist will hit the sides of the north gate."
"Pull down the sides and have him enter."
The Transcendent stands in the broad court before T'ongmyŏng
     Hall.
His height is great.
"Messengers, measure the height of the princess and our son-in-
     law."
"His height is thirty-three heavens and thirty-three feet.
The princess's is twenty-eight lunar mansions and twenty-eight
     feet."
"Then you are indeed a heaven-joined pair,
For the prince who measures to the thirty-three heavens,
Ring the cymbals;

44. This action describes the appearance of the princess as the prototypical
shaman; similar costumes are worn by a shaman when performing this song.
45. Literally, "body governing spirit."

For the princess who measures to the twenty-eight lunar
    mansions,
Ring the large gong."
The king grants them food and garments.
"The son-in-law will have offerings on the road
With many dishes on the large table.
World-Honored Śākyamuni shall receive
The first, second, forty-ninth, and one hundredth day rites.
Herdboy Kangnim on a hill with peaches and plums
Shall receive the seven feet seven inch silk towel,
Grandma praying for merit shall have hemp cloths
At the gate of thorns and of iron.
Grandpa praying for merit shall have
Offerings of *pŏlch'o namhyang*.[46]
And seven sons, two *ton* and one p'un of money offerings."

In the first court, Great King Kuang of Ch'in,[47]
Hear the prayers of my myriad subjects,
Preach the dharma to ferry all living beings across.
Homage to Buddha Amitābha and Bodhisattva Kṣitigarbha.
In the second court, Great King of the First River,
Hear the prayers of my myriad subjects,
Preach the dharma to ferry all living beings across.
Homage to Buddha Amitābha and Bodhisattva Kṣitigarbha.
In the third court, Great King Ti of Sung,
Hear the prayers of my myriad subjects,
Preach the dharma to ferry all living being across.
Homage to Buddha Amitābha and Bodhisattva Kṣitigarbha.
In the fourth court, Great King of Five Offices,
Hear the prayers of my myriad subjects,
Preach the dharma to ferry all living beings across.
Homage to Buddha Amitābha and Bodhisattva Kṣitigarbha.
In the fifth court, Great King Yama,
Hear the prayers of my myriad subjects,

46. Unknown.

47. The ten kings of hell are invoked here. See An Chinho, *Sŏngmun ŭibŏm*
(Pŏmnyunsa, 1966), p. 142, also pp. 180–183, and Stephen F. Teiser, *The Scripture on
the Ten Kings*, Kuroda Institute Studies in East Asian Buddhism no. 9 (Honolulu:
University of Hawaii Press, 1994).

Preach the dharma to ferry all living beings across.
Homage to Buddha Amitābha and Bodhisattva Kṣītigarbha.
In the sixth court, Great King of Transformation,
Hear the prayers of my myriad subjects,
Preach the dharma to ferry all living beings across.
Homage to Buddha Amitābha and Bodhisattva Kṣītigarbha.
In the seventh court, Great King of Mount T'ai,
Hear the prayers of my myriad subjects,
Preach the dharma to ferry all living being across.
Homage to Buddha Amitābha and Bodhisattva Kṣītigarbha.
In the eighth court, Great Impartial King,
Hear the prayers of my myriad subjects,
Preach the dharma to ferry all living beings across.
Homage to Buddha Amitābha and Bodhisattva Kṣītigarbha.
In the ninth court, Great King of the Capital,
Hear the prayers of my myriad subjects,
Preach the dharma to ferry all living beings across.
Homage to Buddha Amitābha and Bodhisattva Kṣītigarbha.
In the tenth court, Great King Who Turns the Wheel of
    Rebirth,
Hear the prayers of my myriad subjects,
Preach the dharma to ferry all living beings across.
Homage to Buddha Amitābha and Bodhisattva Kṣītigarbha.
Hear the prayers of my myriad subjects,
Preach the dharma to ferry all living beings across.
Homage to Buddha Amitābha and Bodhisattva Kṣītigarbha.

Released from three years' mourning,
Consoling the spirits in the underworld,
Released from ancestors' cause of grievance,
From the karma of earthly existence,
The dead man sheds his head cover, the dead woman her yomo
    cap,
With prayers for rebirth in the Land of Happiness,
When you go to the Pure Land,
Open the gate of Knife Hell and the gate of Fire Hell,
Open the gate of Poisonous Snakes and the gate of Ice Cold,
When you go to the Land of Happiness.
The wide dark road leads to hell,

The bright narrow road to the Land of Happiness,
The bright large road to heavenly palace on Milky Way.
Leave aside the wide dark road, take the bright large,
When the road spirit detains you,
Offer the straw sandals from your feet;
When the lady of the grave detains you,
Offer seven outer knots and seven inner knots,
Untie fourteen knots and present them to her.
When an evil spirit detains you,
Offer your undershirt.
When the mountain spirit detains you,
Offer your funeral banners and wooden fan.
When you meet the earth spirit,
Give him upper and lower shrouds,[48]
When you come to the great rocks[49] and sharp rocks,
Offer a bag of your toenails, fingernails, and hair.
When you reach the twelve gates,
Offer three thousand monks' caps.
When you reach the great king's hall,
Transmit meditation practice at Chŏngt'o Monastery
And the cultivator's mystic syllables.
With wet rotten mouth and wet rotten ears,
Invoke the Buddha's name as you go in.
Don't follow the immortal officials robed in blue,
But follow the ones robed in red.
Take the road of the red-robed officials.
Though flourishing rhododendron, azalea, cockscomb, balsam,
Pine, juniper, and cedar thickly line the way,
Don't pluck the flowering twigs,
Don't look behind you,
Go to the high supreme Lotus Terrace,[50]
Seek an immortal lady to become an immortal, and enter the
    Jasper Lake.
Homage to Buddha Amitābha and bodhisattva Kṣitigarbha.

48. Spread on the lower and upper parts of the dead in the coffin.
49. *Chigye* in the original, perhaps a rock that stands on the boundary between
the earth and underworld.
50. Where the Buddha and bodhisattvas sit.

Word by word, line by line, with rotten ears and mouth,
Recite the prayers as you go:
Homage to Buddha Amitābha and Bodhisattva Kṣītigarbha.
First, I cleanse the east, purifying it to a place of worship,[51]
Second, I cleanse the south and obtain coolness,
Third, I cleanse the west and complete the Pure Land,
Fourth, I cleanse the north and become eternally healthy.
As this place of enlightenment is purified, without flaw or
    maculation,
I now keep and recite these sublime mystic syllables,
Vowing to bestow love and compassion and secretly watch over
    everyone.
Bodhisattva Who Observes the Sounds of the World
With a Thousand Hands and Eyes!
Homage to Buddha Amitābha,
Homage to Buddha Amitābha,
Homage to Buddha Amitābha.
I lead the former dead, later dead, all the dead ancestors,
Generation after generation, son after son,
This is the day they go to the Land of Happiness.

P L

51. See *Sŏngmun ŭibŏm*, p. 97; translated in Robert Buswell Jr., *The Zen Monastic Experience* (Princeton: Princeton University Press, 1992), p. 239.

An Minyŏng (fl. 1870–1880). A secondary son and professional singer, he is a coeditor of *Sourcebook of Songs* (*Kagok wŏllyu*, 1876). He is a poet of flowers and addressed ten songs to plum blossoms.

Chingak, National Preceptor (Hyesim, 1178–1234). He became a monk under Chinul and succeeded him at Susŏn Monastery. Chingak is a posthumous epithet.

Cho Chonsŏng (1553–1627). A disciple of Sŏng Hon (1535–1598) and Pak Chihwa (1513–1592), Cho was a graduate of the 1590 examination (*munkwa*). During the Japanese invasion he went to Ming China to plead for a military reinforcement; during the Manchu invasion he served the crown prince (1627). His four *sijo* are preserved in the *Songs of Korea* (*Haedong kayo*, 1763, 1770).

Cho Hŏn (1544–1592). A disciple of Yi I (1536–1384) and Sŏng Hon and a graduate of the 1567 examination, he proposed strengthening the national defense when the Japanese envoy came in 1591, but the factious court ignored him. During the invasion he recruited the Righteous Army and recaptured Ch'ŏngju but was killed in action at a battle in Kŭmsan. He is enshrined in the Confucian Temple.

Cho Hwi (fl. 1568–1608). Little is known about his career.

Cho Myŏnghŭi (1697–1756). A graduate of the 1731 examination, he served as mayor of Seoul.

Cho Sik (1501–1572). He never took office and lived an idyllic life on Mount Turyu (Chiri). The sijo presented here expresses his sorrow over the death of King Myŏngjong (1545–1567).

Ch'oe Ch'iwŏn (b. 857). In 868 he left for T'ang China where after six years of study he won the "presented scholar" degree. When the Huang Ch'ao rebellion broke out (874), he was secretary under the military commander Kao Pien. He returned to Korea in 885 and is said to have spent his last years at Haein Monastery. He was posthumously honored as marquis (1023), and his collected works are published in China. The *Anthology of*

Korean Literature in Chinese (*Tong munsŏn,* 1478) preserves 146 of his poems.

Ch'oe Kinam (seventeenth century). A poet of common origin, he organized a poetry club and led a quiet life.

Ch'ŏn Kŭm (dates unknown). Little is known about her except for a single sijo preserved in the *Hwawŏn akpo,* an anonymous anthology of 650 sijo compiled at the end of the nineteenth century.

Chŏng Chisang (d. 1135). A graduate of the 1114 examination, he held a series of court posts, including that of censor (1129). In 1135 he was implicated in a rebellion and executed.

Chŏng Ch'ŏl (1537–1594). Chŏng's political career was turbulent owing to party strife at court. He was subtle in weaving words together and relied for effect on a cunning juxtaposition that presented a familiar word as new. The Sŏngju edition of 1747, the most complete edition of his *Pine River Anthology,* contains five kasa and seventy-nine sijo. For more see *Pine River and Lone Peak* (Honolulu, 1991), pp. 43–86. "Song of Longing" (*Sa miin kok*) and "Continued Song of Longing" (*Sok miin kok*) are allegorical poems written around 1585–1587 when Chŏng was forced by his political foes to retire to the countryside. In both poems he compares his loyalty to King Sŏnjo with that of a faithful wife longing for her absent husband or beloved. For more see *Pine River and Lone Peak,* pp. 14–16. "Little Odes on Mount Star" (*Sŏngsan pyŏlgok*) was written in praise of the elegant life that Kim Sŏngwŏn (1515–1598) had established at the Mist Settling Hall and Resting Shadow Arbor on Mount Star in South Chŏlla. For more on this work see *Pine River and Lone Peak,* pp. 16–18.

Chŏng Mongju (1337–1392). A statesman, scholar, and diplomat who often represented Koryŏ in China and Japan, Chŏng was a pillar of the declining Koryŏ dynasty. Yi Sŏnggye and his fifth son, Yi Pangwŏn, in an attempt to sway Chŏng's loyalty, held a banquet in his honor where he sang this song to express his unshakable determination. Thereupon Yi Pangwŏn sent assassins to have Chŏng murdered on his way home.

Chŏng Sŏ (c. 1151–1170). The author of the Koryŏ song "Regret" is a favorite courtier of King Injong. History describes him as talented but frivolous.

Chŏng Yagyong (1762–1836). A great champion of practical learning, he was strongly influenced by Catholicism and took John as his baptismal name. For his treatise on land, well-field system, tools and techniques, wicked petty officials, Korea's northern border regions, music, and what the principle and material force debate is all about, see *Sourcebook of Korean Civilization* 2:64–69, 69–71, 100–108, 211–214, 233–235, 242–245, 269–271.

Chŏnggam, Great Master (1533–1609). A disciple of Great Master Sŏsan (1520–1604), he became a monk at age fourteen.

from 1864 to 1910, was published in 1955. Hwang was posthumously honored in 1962.

Hwang O (dates unknown). Nothing is known about him.

Im Che (1549–1597). A disciple of Sŏng Hon and a graduate of the 1577 examination, he scorned factional strife and led a retired life. His poetry is known for its bold extravagance. Tradition has it that the song presented here was composed when he visited the tomb of Hwang Chini to pay tribute to her memory.

Im Ŏngnyŏng (1469–1568). A graduate of the 1515 examination, he shunned the corrupt world of politics until 1551 when he began to hold office, including the governorship of Kangwŏn province.

Kil Chae (1353–1419). After the fall of Koryŏ, he refused the honors bestowed upon him by the new dynasty, lived concealed in the countryside, and devoted himself to nurturing disciples. Moved by the tears of things, he composed the sijo cited here.

Kim Ch'anghyŏp (1651–1708). A graduate of the 1682 examination, he consistently declined offers from the court, especially after his own father, Kim Suhang, was ordered to commit suicide in 1689. Kim's reputation as a man of letters and thinker has never been disputed.

Kim Ch'ŏnt'aek (c. 1725–1776). A professional singer and a policeman, he compiled the first anthology of sijo, *Songs of Green Hills* (*Ch'ŏnggu yŏngŏn*, 1728). *Songs of Korea* contains fifty-seven of his sijo.

Kim Koengp'il (1454–1504). A graduate of the 1480 examination, he was implicated in the 1504 purge and was executed. Versed in the Human Nature and Principle learning (*sŏngnihak*), he nurtured a number of eminent scholars. He is enshrined in the Confucian Temple.

Kim Ku (1488–1534). When King Chungjong made a surprise visit to the Office of Special Advisers, Kim composed the song presented here to wish the king long life.

Kim Kwanguk (1580–1656). A graduate of the 1606 examination, he served King Injo and went to Peking as an envoy (1654). He is the author of a cycle of fourteen sijo, *Songs of Chestnut Village* (*Yulli yugok*), in praise of a simple life.

Kim Pyŏngyŏn (Kim Ip, 1807–1863), alias Kim Sakkat (Kim the Bamboo Hat). As a magistrate of Sŏnch'ŏn, Kim's grandfather, Kim Iksun, surrendered to a rebel peasant army in the northwest, was captured, sent to the capital for trial, and executed outside the west gate in Seoul on a charge of high treason (April 19, 1812). As a consequence, his male descendents were prohibited from holding public office. Thus marginalized as the grandson of a rebel, Kim became a bamboo-hatted vagabond poet and left behind some two hundred poems in Chinese—some puerile, some satiric, some comic. Yi Munyŏl's *The Poet* (London, 1995) is a fictional biography of Kim.

Kim Sangyong (1561–1637). A disciple of Sŏng Hon, Kim was a graduate of the 1582 examination. When Kanghwa Island fell into the hands of the invading Manchu, he climbed atop the south gate of the fortress and blew himself to pieces with gunpowder. He left behind some twenty sijo.

Kim Sisŭp (1435–1493). An infant prodigy, he was tested by King Sejong and awarded a royal present. At the news of Sejo's usurpation (1455), Kim shaved his head and became a tireless traveler. Versed in the meditation school of Buddhism and Taoism, he overawed his rivals. He is also the author of a collection of five tales of wonder, *New Stories from Gold Turtle Mountain* (*Kŭmo sinhwa*).

Kim Sŏnggi (c. 1725–1776). First an archer, then a master of the black zither and other musical instruments, Kim was known for his singing voice.

Kim Sujang (b. 1690). A clerk during the reign of Sukchong and a professional singer, he compiled *Songs of Korea* (1763, 1770), in which he is represented by 117 sijo.

Kim Yŏng (fl. 1776–1800). He passed the military examination and reached the rank of minister of punishments. He left seven sijo songs.

Kim Yuk (1580–1658). In 1644 he imported European books on the calendar and algebra; in 1651 as chief state counselor he encouraged land reform and copper cash. For more on Kim's contribution to the growing market economy see *Sourcebook of Korean Civilization* 2:73–74 and 110–112.

King Mu of Paekche (r. 600–614). The thirtieth ruler of Paekche, he often harassed Silla's borders. In 642 he sent an envoy to T'ang China and was enfeoffed by the first emperor as "King of Taebang Commandery and King of Paekche." He dispatched the monk Kwallŭk (J. Kanroku) to Japan with books on Buddhism, astronomy, geography, and the calendar. From 630 on he was actively repairing palaces or building monasteries. King Mu is the author of "Song of Sŏdong" (c. 600); an alternate reading has the princess being carried to Sŏdong's arms.

Kwŏn Homun (1532–1587). A disciple of Yi Hwang, he passed the 1561 examination but did not take office and lived below Mount Ch'ŏngsong all his life. He is the author of a cycle of eighteen sijo (*Hangŏ sipp'al kok*).

Kwŏn P'il (1569–1612). A disciple of Chŏng Ch'ŏl, he had no interest in a worldly career and did not take examination. He was poor but managed to spend his life with wine and poetry. At one time, urged by poet friends, he exchanged poetry with a Ming envoy to Korea—then considered the highest recognition and honor.

Kyerang (Yi Hyanggŭm, 1513–1550). With the pen name "Plum Window," she was a famous entertainer from Puan, North Chŏlla, versed in poetry both in Chinese and Korean, the black zither, and dance. She left some seventy pieces in Korean and Chinese, but her collected works are no longer extant.

Myŏngok (late sixteenth century). Little is known about her, except that she was an entertainer from Suwŏn, with the professional name "Bright Jade."

Naong, Master (Hyesun, 1320–1376). At the age of twenty he became a monk and then traveled to Yüan China where he received the dharma transmission from P'ing-shan Ch'u-lin of the Lin-chi school. Returning to Korea in 1350, he introduced the meditation of observing the critical phrase (*kanhwa*) and the practice of meditation with the invocation of the Buddha's name. "Song of the Pure Land" was orally transmitted until the early eighteenth century.

Nŭngun (dates unknown). Little seems to be known about her.

O Cham (fl. 1274–1308). A sycophant of King Ch'ungnyŏl and the putative author of "The Turkish Bakery."

Pak Hyogwan (c. 1850–1880). A professional singer and compiler, together with An Minyŏng, of the *Sourcebook of Songs* (1876). He was a favorite of Taewŏngun (Prince of the Great Court, 1820–1898), King Kojong's father, and left thirteen sijo.

Pak Illo (1561–1643). Pak joined an army in 1592 to fight the Japanese invaders. In 1599 he passed the military examination and became myriarch at Chorap'o, a garrison on Kŏje Island. In 1605 he was named a shipmaster in Pusan but ended his military career in the same year. Pak is the author of sixty-eight sijo and seven kasa. For more on Pak see *Pine River and Lone Peak*, pp. 87–140.

Pongnim, Prince (1619–1659). The second son of King Injo, he ascended the throne as Hyojong (r. 1649–1659). He spent eight years of his youth as a hostage in Ch'ing China and wanted to erase the shame of Manchu subjugation but died before realizing his dream.

Pyŏn Wŏngyu (fl. 1881–1884). An interpreter of Chinese who accompanied the Korean ambassador Kim Yunsik to China in his talks with Li Hung-chang (1823–1901). He was known for his poetry and calligraphy.

Sinch'ung (fl. 737–757). The author of the Silla song "Regret," he rose to be prime minister in 757 and later became a monk and prayed for the soul of King Hyosŏng.

Sin Hŭm (1566–1628). A graduate of the 1586 examination, Sin reached the rank of chief state counselor. During the Japanese invasion he served both Sin Ip (1546–1592) and Chŏng Ch'ŏl. He is known as an accomplished scholar of Neo-Confucianism of the Ch'eng-Chu school and a writer in Chinese.

Sin Saimdang, Lady (1504–1552). Mother of Yi I (1536–1584), a Neo-Confucian philosopher, she was known for her poetry, for painting landscape, grapes, and insects, and, above all, as a paragon of the wise and caring mother.

Sŏ Kyŏngdŏk (1489–1546). A tireless traveler and thinker who devoted his life to the study of Neo-Confucian metaphysics. Although he passed the examination, he decided to live a retired life at Hwadam, outside of the east gate of Kaesŏng. He is said to have withstood the temptation of Hwang Chini, the most famous entertainer and woman poet of the time; one source says she was his pupil. For Sŏ's philosophical position see *Sourcebook of Korean Civilization* 1:607–610.

Sŏng Hon (1535–1598). A man of wide learning who refused public life. During the Japanese invasion, however, summoned by the crown prince, he served the government. Of his philosophical writings the most famous is a series of correspondence with Yi I on Neo-Confucian metaphysics; see *Sourcebook of Korean Civilization* 1:633–641.

Song Ikp'il (1534–1599). As a secondary son he gave up an official career and befriended Yi I and Sŏng Hon to debate the Human Nature and Principle learning. Also an accomplished writer, he nurtured latecomers such as Kim Changsaeng (1548–1631), an expert in the rites, at the foot of Mount Kwibong in Koyang, near Seoul.

Sŏng Kan (1427–1456). Upon learning of the forced abdication of Tanjong in 1455, he hastened to Yŏngwŏl where the deposed king was imprisoned. At the news of his murder, Sŏng withdrew to a remote mountain and observed two years' mourning.

Sŏng Sammun (1418–1456). One of the six martyred ministers of Tanjong. When Sejo forced the abdication of his fourteen-year-old cousin, Sŏng and others plotted his restoration. Sŏng was tortured and quartered; at a crucial moment, he expressed his undying loyalty to the memory of his lord.

Song Sun (1493–1583). He went to Ming China as an envoy in 1547, then retired to Tamyang, South Chŏlla, and led a quiet life.

Sŏngjong, King (1456–1494, r. 1469–1494). The ninth king of Chosŏn, he addressed the song presented here to Yu Hoin (1445–1494), assistant section chief of the Ministry of Works, his favorite courtier.

Sŏsan, Great Master (Hyujŏng, 1520–1604). He passed the monk examination in 1549 and in 1592, under royal orders, took command of the monk soldiers. Because of his successful military campaigns, he became a folk hero. He tried to unify the meditation and doctrinal schools to revitalize Korean Buddhism. For more see *Sourcebook of Korean Civilization* 1.658–665.

T'aego, National Preceptor (Pou, 1301–1382). He became a monk at age thirteen and passed the monk's examination in 1325. In 1346 he went to Yüan China and became a master of the Lin-chi school of meditation. On returning to Korea in 1348, he became royal preceptor of King Kongmin and then national preceptor.

Tŭgo or Tŭgogok (fl. 692–702). A member of the *hwarang* headed by Knight Chukchi (or Chungman). The ode presented here was composed to lament the knight's death.

U T'ak (1263–1342). He studied the Neo-Confucianism of the Ch'eng-Chu school and was versed in the *Book of Changes*. Two songs are attributed to him.

Wŏlmyŏng, Master (c. 742–765). Monk, poet, and member of the *hwarang*, leaders of the knights in Silla, he is the author of two Silla songs: "Song of Tuṣita Heaven" and "Requiem for the Dead Sister."

Wŏn Ch'ŏnsŏk (c. 1390–1410). A tutor of Yi Pangwŏn, the future king of Chosŏn. The song presented here is one of the two attributed to him.

Yejong, King (1079–1122, r. 1105–1122). The sixteenth ruler of Koryŏ, he delighted in exchanging poems in Chinese with his courtiers and wrote "Dirge for Two Generals," a hyangga song.

Yi Chehyŏn (1287–1367). A graduate of the 1301 examination at the age of fifteen, he went to Yüan China at least six times to accompany the Korean kings in residence at the Mongol court. Versed in Chinese tonal patterns and prosody, he excelled in the "Music Bureau" songs and "lyrics" (*tz'u*). He also translated into Chinese nine folk songs current in his day under the title *A Small Collection of Folk Songs* (*So akpu*). His collected works, first published in 1363, were reprinted in 1432, 1693, and 1814.

Yi Chŏngbo (1693–1766). A graduate of the 1732 examination, he excelled in calligraphy and poetry in Chinese and the vernacular. He left seventy-eight sijo.

Yi Chono (1341–1371). He passed the 1360 examination. The allusion to clouds refers to villainous courtiers pursuing fame and wealth rather than serving the country and people.

Yi Hwang (1501–1571). Perhaps the most renowned Neo-Confucian philosopher in Korea; his sijo cycle (1565) praised, and moralized upon, the beauties of Tosan in North Kyŏngsang. For his works see *Sourcebook of Korean Civilization* 1:471, 506–510, and 613–633.

Yi I (1536–1584). Together with Yi Hwang, one of the celebrated Neo-Confucian philosophers in Korea, he was also active in public service. His sijo cycle centers on Mount Ko in the Suyang Mountains in Haeju. The first is a prologue; the rest of the nine songs cover the four seasons of the year. The nine place names supply images for poetic amplification. For his works in politics and economy see *Sourcebook of Korean Civilization* 1:589, 633–641. For his letters to Sŏng Hon see 1:511–514. For his Neo-Confucian curriculum see *Sources of Korean Tradition* 2:35–36; on community compacts see 2:145–157.

Yi Illo (1151–1220). Poet, historian, and scholar, Yi excelled in verse and prose. In 1180 he placed first in the examination and served fourteen years in the academy of letters and the office of historiography, then as head of the royal archives. Except for his *Jottings to Break Up Idleness* (*P'ahan chip*, 1260), the first literary miscellany in Korea, his two other collections are no longer extant. Anthologies preserve 129 of Yi's poems. For more see *A Korean Storyteller's Miscellany*, pp. 3–56.

Yi Kae (1417–1456). One of the six martyred ministers of Tanjong and a graduate of the 1447 examination, he tried to restore Tanjong and was tortured to death by Sejo (1455–1468).

Yi Kyubo (1168–1241). A graduate of the 1190 examination, Yi accompanied the court to Kanghwa Island during the Mongol invasion and rose to be first privy counselor. His collected works (1241, 1251) provide invaluable information on the history of the Three Kingdoms and Koryŏ; for example, chapter 3 contains the "Lay of King Tongmyŏng," the foundation myth of Koguryŏ. His works contain some two thousand poems.

Yi Myŏnghan (1595–1645). A graduate of the 1616 examination, as an opponent to peace with the Manchus he was transported to Shenyang (Mukden). He was versed in the Human Nature and Principle learning.

Yi Saek (1328–1396). He passed the examination at the Eastern Expedition field headquarters to qualify for the metropolitan and palace examinations at the Mongol capital (1353–1354). He then served in the Hanlin Academy and Historiography Academy. "The tree of the perfect plum" in the song presented here refers to the declining Koryŏ royal house.

Yi Sunsin (1545–1598). A famous Korean admiral who with his "turtle ship" defeated the Japanese navy during their invasion in 1592–1598. For the Koreans he is more than an icon–he is a constellation, high in the sky, to be admired and emulated. For more on Yi see *The Record of the Black Dragon Year* (Seoul and Honolulu, 2000).

Yi T'aek (1651–1719). He passed the military examination of 1676 and served as navy commander. Two sijo are attributed to him.

Yi Tal (fl. 1568–1608). Together with two other poets he was known as one of the Three T'ang-Style Masters who emulated the poetry of High T'ang.

Yi Yŏng (1615–1637). During the Manchu invasion he fought on Kanghwa Island. After its fall, while taking refuge with his family, his party met with enemy soldiers who killed his father. Trying to avoid capture, his mother jumped into a fire. Yi rescued her and tried to escape with her on his back but was killed by an enemy arrow. Both his wife and his sister-in-law committed suicide.

Yŏngjae, Monk (fl.785–798). A Silla monk who believed in the power of poetry to touch the heart. In "Meeting with Bandits" he transcends the moment to find a truth that he and the bandits can share. Thus his song, enabling the bandits to see life more clearly, is more hermeneutic than therapeutic in function.

Yu Mongin (1559–1623). A graduate of the 1589 examination, but because of his frivolous character his political career was checkered at best. Implicated in a revolt in 1623, he and his son were executed. He is the author of a collection of unofficial historical narratives.

Yu Ŭngbu (d. 1456). One of the six martyred ministers of Tanjong and a military official, Yu was tortured to death for his role in plotting the restoration of the deposed boy king.

Yun Sŏndo (1587–1671). Generally regarded as the most accomplished poet in the sijo form, Yun left seventy-five songs. His political career was turbulent, and he spent fourteen years in exile. He is known for "Songs of Five Friends" (1642), a sijo cycle of six songs, and "The Angler's Calendar" (1651), a cycle of forty songs. For more on Yun see *Pine River and Lone Peak*, pp. 141–168.

Yun Tusŏ (b. 1668). Writer, painter, and Yun Sŏndo's great-grandson, he passed the 1693 examination. A number of his paintings survive.

Yungch'ŏn, Master (c. 579–632). His "Song of the Comet" (594) worked a miracle: it removed a comet that had ominously appeared in the sky.

INDEX OF FIRST LINES

BIBLIOGRAPHY

Chang, Kang-i Sun and Haun Saussy, eds. *Women Writers of Traditional China: An Anthology of Poetry and Criticism*. Stanford: Stanford University Press, 1999.

Ch'oe, Yŏngho, Peter H. Lee, and Wm. Theodore de Bary, eds. *Sources of Korean Tradition: From the Sixteenth to the Twentieth Centuries*. New York: Columbia University Press, 2001.

Kim Jong-gil. *Slow Chrysanthemums: Classical Korean Poems in Chinese*. London: Anvil, 1987.

Lee, Peter H. *Celebration of Continuity: Themes in Classic East Asian Poetry*. Cambridge: Harvard University Press, 1979.

—— *A Korean Storyteller's Miscellany*. Princeton: Princeton University Press, 1989.

—— *Pine River and Lone Peak: An Anthology of Three Chosŏn Dynasty Poets*. Honolulu: University of Hawaii Press, 1991.

—— *The Record of the Black Dragon Year*. Seoul: Institute of Korean Culture, Korea University, and Honolulu: Center for Korean Studies, 2000.

—— *Songs of Flying Dragons: A Critical Reading*. Cambridge: Harvard University Press, 1975.

Lee, Peter H., ed. *Anthology of Korean Literature: From Early Times to the Nineteenth Century*. Honolulu: University of Hawaii Press, 1981; rev. ed. 1990.

—— *Myths of Korea*. Somerset and Seoul: Jimmondang International, 2000.

—— *Sourcebook of Korean Civilization*. 2 vols. New York: Columbia University Press, 1993–1996.

Lee, Peter H. and Wm. Theodore de Bary, eds. *Sources of Korean Tradition: From Early Times Through the Sixteenth Century*. New York: Columbia University Press, 1997.

McCann, David R. *Early Korean Literature: Selections and Introductions*. New York: Columbia University Press, 2000.

O'Rourke, Kevin. *Singing Like a Cricket, Hooting Like an Owl: Selected Poems of Yi Kyu-bo*. Ithaca: Cornell East Asian Program, 1995.

Rutt, Richard. *The Bamboo Grove: An Introduction to Sijo*. Berkeley: University of California Press, 1971.

TRANSLATIONS FROM THE ASIAN CLASSICS

Major Plays of Chikamatsu, tr. Donald Keene 1961

Four Major Plays of Chikamatsu, tr. Donald Keene. Paperback ed. only. 1961; rev. ed. 1997

Records of the Grand Historian of China, translated from the Shih chi of Ssu-ma Ch'ien, tr. Burton Watson, 2 vols. 1961

Instructions for Practical Living and Other Neo-Confucian Writings by Wang Yang-ming, tr. Wing-tsit Chan 1963

Hsün Tzu: Basic Writings, tr. Burton Watson, paperback ed. only. 1963; rev. ed. 1996

Chuang Tzu: Basic Writings, tr. Burton Watson, paperback ed. only. 1964; rev. ed. 1996

The Mahāābhārata, tr. Chakravarthi V. Narasimhan. Also in paperback ed. 1965; rev. ed. 1997

The Manyōshū, Nippon Gakujutsu Shinkōkai edition 1965

Su Tung-p'o: Selections from a Sung Dynasty Poet, tr. Burton Watson. Also in paperback ed. 1965

Bhartrihari: Poems, tr. Barbara Stoler Miller. Also in paperback ed. 1967

Basic Writings of Mo Tzu, Hsün Tzu, and Han Fei Tzu, tr. Burton Watson. Also in separate paperback eds. 1967

The Awakening of Faith, Attributed to Aśvaghosha, tr. Yoshito S. Hakeda. Also in paperback ed. 1967

Reflections on Things at Hand: The Neo-Confucian Anthology, comp. Chu Hsi and Lü Tsu-ch'ien, tr. Wing-tsit Chan 1967

The Platform Sutra of the Sixth Patriarch, tr. Philip B. Yampolsky. Also in paperback ed. 1967

Essays in Idleness: The Tsurezuregusa of Kenkō, tr. Donald Keene. Also in paperback ed. 1967

The Pillow Book of Sei Shōnagon, tr. Ivan Morris, 2 vols. 1967

Two Plays of Ancient India: The Little Clay Cart and the Minister's Seal, tr. J. A. B. van Buitenen 1968

The Complete Works of Chuang Tzu, tr. Burton Watson 1968

The Romance of the Western Chamber (Hsi Hsiang chi), tr. S. I. Hsiung. Also in paperback ed. 1968

The Manyōshū, Nippon Gakujutsu Shinkōkai edition. Paperback ed. only. 1969

Records of the Historian: Chapters from the Shih chi of Ssu-ma Ch'ien, tr. Burton Watson. Paperback ed. only. 1969

Cold Mountain: 100 Poems by the T'ang Poet Han-shan, tr. Burton Watson. Also in paperback ed. 1970

Twenty Plays of the Nō Theatre, ed. Donald Keene. Also in paperback ed. 1970

Chūshingura: The Treasury of Loyal Retainers, tr. Donald Keene. Also in paperback ed. 1971; rev. ed. 1997

The Zen Master Hakuin: Selected Writings, tr. Philip B. Yampolsky 1971

Chinese Rhyme-Prose: Poems in the Fu Form from the Han and Six Dynasties Periods, tr. Burton Watson. Also in paperback ed. 1971

Kūkai: Major Works, tr. Yoshito S. Hakeda. Also in paperback ed. 1972

The Old Man Who Does as He Pleases: Selections from the Poetry and Prose of Lu Yu, tr. Burton Watson 1973

The Lion's Roar of Queen Śrīmālā, tr. Alex and Hideko Wayman 1974

Courtier and Commoner in Ancient China: Selections from the History of the Former Han by Pan Ku, tr. Burton Watson. Also in paperback ed. 1974

Japanese Literature in Chinese, vol. 1: Poetry and Prose in Chinese by Japanese Writers of the Early Period, tr. Burton Watson 1975

Japanese Literature in Chinese, vol. 2: Poetry and Prose in Chinese by Japanese Writers of the Later Period, tr. Burton Watson 1976

Scripture of the Lotus Blossom of the Fine Dharma, tr. Leon Hurvitz. Also in paperback ed. 1976

Love Song of the Dark Lord: Jayadeva's Gītagovinda, tr. Barbara Stoler Miller. Also in paperback ed. Cloth ed. includes critical text of the Sanskrit. 1977; rev. ed. 1997

Ryōkan: Zen Monk-Poet of Japan, tr. Burton Watson 1977

Calming the Mind and Discerning the Real: From the Lam rim chen mo of Tsom-kha-pa, tr. Alex Wayman 1978

The Hermit and the Love-Thief: Sanskrit Poems of Bhartrihari and Bilhama, tr. Barbara Stoler Miller 1978

The Lute: Kao Ming's P'i-p'a chi, tr. Jean Mulligan. Also in paperback ed. 1980

A Chronicle of Gods and Sovereigns: Jinnō Shōtōki of Kitabatake Chikafusa, tr. H. Paul Varley 1980

Among the Flowers: The Hua-chien chi, tr. Lois Fusek 1982

Grass Hill: Poems and Prose by the Japanese Monk Gensei, tr. Burton Watson 1983

Doctors, Diviners, and Magicians of Ancient China: Biographies of Fang-shih, tr. Kenneth J. DeWoskin. Also in paperback ed. 1983

Theater of Memory: The Plays of Kālidāsa, ed. Barbara Stoler Miller. Also in paperback ed. 1984

The Columbia Book of Chinese Poetry: From Early Times to the Thirteenth Century, ed. and tr. Burton Watson. Also in paperback ed. 1984

Poems of Love and War: From the Eight Anthologies and the Ten Long Poems of Classical Tamil, tr. A. K. Ramanujan. Also in paperback ed. 1985

The Bhagavad Gita: Krishna's Counsel in Time of War, tr. Barbara Stoler Miller 1986

The Columbia Book of Later Chinese Poetry, ed. and tr. Jonathan Chaves. Also in paperback ed. 1986

The Tso Chuan: Selections from China's Oldest Narrative History, tr. Burton Watson 1989

Waiting for the Wind: Thirty-six Poets of Japan's Late Medieval Age, tr. Steven Carter 1989

Selected Writings of Nichiren, ed. Philip B. Yampolsky 1990

Saigyō, Poems of a Mountain Home, tr. Burton Watson 1990

The Book of Lieh Tzu: A Classic of the Tao, tr. A. C. Graham. Morningside ed. 1990

The Tale of an Anklet: An Epic of South India—The Cilappatikāram of Ilamkō Atikal, tr. R. Parthasarathy 1993

Waiting for the Dawn: A Plan for the Prince, tr. and introduction by Wm. Theodore de Bary 1993

Yoshitsune and the Thousand Cherry Trees: A Masterpiece of the Eighteenth-Century Japanese Puppet Theater, tr., annotated, and with introduction by Stanleigh H. Jones, Jr. 1993

The Lotus Sutra, tr. Burton Watson. Also in paperback ed. 1993

The Classic of Changes: A New Translation of the I Ching as Interpreted by Wang Bi, tr. Richard John Lynn 1994

Beyond Spring: Tz'u Poems of the Sung Dynasty, tr. Julie Landau 1994

The Columbia Anthology of Traditional Chinese Literature, ed. Victor H. Mair 1994

Scenes for Mandarins: The Elite Theater of the Ming, tr. Cyril Birch 1995

Letters of Nichiren, ed. Philip B. Yampolsky; tr. Burton Watson et al. 1996

Unforgotten Dreams: Poems by the Zen Monk Shōtetsu, tr. Steven D. Carter 1997

The Vimalakirti Sutra, tr. Burton Watson 1997

Japanese and Chinese Poems to Sing: The Wakan rōei shū, tr. J. Thomas Rimer and Jonathan Chaves 1997

A Tower for the Summer Heat, Li Yu, tr. Patrick Hanan 1998

Traditional Japanese Theater: An Anthology of Plays, Karen Brazell 1998

The Original Analects: Sayings of Confucius and His Successors (0479–0249), E. Bruce Brooks and A. Taeko Brooks 1998

The Classic of the Way and Virtue: A New Translation of the Tao-te ching *of Laozi as Interpreted by Wang Bi*, tr. Richard John Lynn 1999

The Four Hundred Songs of War and Wisdom: An Anthology of Poems from Classical Tamil, The Puranāmūru, eds. and trans. George L. Hart and Hank Heifetz 1999

Original Tao: Inward Training (Nei-yeh) *and the Foundations of Taoist Mysticism*, by Harold D. Roth 1999

Lao Tzu's Tao Te Ching: *A Translation of the Startling New Documents Found at Guodian*, Robert G. Henricks 2000

The Shorter Columbia Anthology of Traditional Chinese Literature, ed. Victor H. Mair 2000

Mistress and Maid (Jiaohongji) by Meng Chengshun, tr. Cyril Birch 2001

Chikamatsu: Five Late Plays, tr. and ed. C. Andrew Gerstle

The Essential Lotus: Selections from the Lotus Sutra, tr. Burton Watson 2002

Early Modern Japanese Literature: An Anthology, 1600–1900, ed. Haruo Shirane 2002

Zhuangzhi: Basic Writings, tr. and ed. Burton Watson 2003

MODERN ASIAN LITERATURE

Modern Japanese Drama: An Anthology, ed. and tr. Ted. Takaya. Also in paperback ed. 1979

Mask and Sword: Two Plays for the Contemporary Japanese Theater, by Yamazaki Masakazu, tr. J. Thomas Rimer 1980

Yokomitsu Riichi, Modernist, Dennis Keene 1980

Nepali Visions, Nepali Dreams: The Poetry of Laxmiprasad Devkota, tr. David Rubin 1980

Literature of the Hundred Flowers, vol. 1: *Criticism and Polemics*, ed. Hualing Nieh 1981

Literature of the Hundred Flowers, vol. 2: *Poetry and Fiction*, ed. Hualing Nieh 1981

Modern Chinese Stories and Novellas, 1919 1949, ed. Joseph S. M. Lau, C. T. Hsia, and Leo Ou-fan Lee. Also in paperback ed. 1984

A View by the Sea, by Yasuoka Shōtarō, tr. Kären Wigen Lewis 1984

Other Worlds: Arishima Takeo and the Bounds of Modern Japanese Fiction, by Paul Anderer 1984

Selected Poems of Sŏ Chōngju, tr. with introduction by David R. McCann 1989

The Sting of Life: Four Contemporary Japanese Novelists, by Van C. Gessel 1989

Stories of Osaka Life, by Oda Sakunosuke, tr. Burton Watson 1990

The Bodhisattva, or Samantabhadra, by Ishikawa Jun, tr. with introduction by William Jefferson Tyler 1990

The Travels of Lao Ts'an, by Liu T'ieh-yün, tr. Harold Shadick. Morningside ed. 1990

Three Plays by Kōbō Abe, tr. with introduction by Donald Keene 1993

The Columbia Anthology of Modern Chinese Literature, ed. Joseph S. M. Lau and Howard Goldblatt 1995

Modern Japanese Tanka, ed. and tr. by Makoto Ueda 1996

Masaoka Shiki: Selected Poems, ed. and tr. by Burton Watson 1997

Writing Women in Modern China: An Anthology of Women's Literature from the Early Twentieth Century, ed. and tr. by Amy D. Dooling and Kristina M. Torgeson 1998

American Stories, by Nagai Kafū, tr. Mitsuko Iriye 2000

The Paper Door and Other Stories, by Shiga Naoya, tr. Lane Dunlop 2001

Grass for My Pillow, by Saiichi Maruya, tr. Dennis Keene 2002

STUDIES IN ASIAN CULTURE

The Nnin War: History of Its Origins and Background, with a Selective Translation of the Chronicle of ōnin, by H. Paul Varley 1967

Chinese Government in Ming Times: Seven Studies, ed. Charles O. Hucker 1969

The Actors' Analects (Yakusha Rongo), ed. and tr. by Charles J. Dunn and Bungō Torigoe 1969

Self and Society in Ming Thought, by Wm. Theodore de Bary and the Conference on Ming Thought. Also in paperback ed. 1970

A History of Islamic Philosophy, by Majid Fakhry, 2d ed. 1983

Phantasies of a Love Thief: The CaurapanatcāŚikā Attributed to Bilhama, by Barbara Stoler Miller 1971

Iqbal: Poet-Philosopher of Pakistan, ed. Hafeez Malik 1971

The Golden Tradition: An Anthology of Urdu Poetry, ed. and tr. Ahmed Ali. Also in paperback ed. 1973

Conquerors and Confucians: Aspects of Political Change in Late Yüan China, by John W. Dardess 1973

The Unfolding of Neo-Confucianism, by Wm. Theodore de Bary and the Conference on Seventeenth-Century Chinese Thought. Also in paperback ed. 1975

To Acquire Wisdom: The Way of Wang Yang-ming, by Julia Ching 1976

Gods, Priests, and Warriors: The Bhṛgus of the Mahābhārata, by Robert P. Goldman 1977

Mei Yao-ch'en and the Development of Early Sung Poetry, by Jonathan Chaves 1976

The Legend of Semimaru, Blind Musician of Japan, by Susan Matisoff 1977
Sir Sayyid Ahmad Khan and Muslim Modernization in India and Pakistan, by Hafeez Malik 1980
The Khilafat Movement: Religious Symbolism and Political Mobilization in India, by Gail Minault 1982
The World of K'ung Shang-jen: A Man of Letters in Early Ch'ing China, by Richard Strassberg 1983
The Lotus Boat: The Origins of Chinese Tz'u Poetry in T'ang Popular Culture, by Marsha L. Wagner 1984
Expressions of Self in Chinese Literature, ed. Robert E. Hegel and Richard C. Hessney 1985
Songs for the Bride: Women's Voices and Wedding Rites of Rural India, by W. G. Archer; eds. Barbara Stoler Miller and Mildred Archer 1986
The Confucian Kingship in Korea: Yǎngjo and the Politics of Sagacity, by JaHyun Kim Haboush 1988

COMPANIONS TO ASIAN STUDIES

Approaches to the Oriental Classics, ed. Wm. Theodore de Bary 1959
Early Chinese Literature, by Burton Watson. Also in paperback ed. 1962
Approaches to Asian Civilizations, eds. Wm. Theodore de Bary and Ainslie T. Embree 1964
The Classic Chinese Novel: A Critical Introduction, by C. T. Hsia. Also in paperback ed. 1968
Chinese Lyricism: Shih Poetry from the Second to the Twelfth Century, tr. Burton Watson. Also in paperback ed. 1971
A Syllabus of Indian Civilization, by Leonard A. Gordon and Barbara Stoler Miller 1971
Twentieth-Century Chinese Stories, ed. C. T. Hsia and Joseph S. M. Lau. Also in paperback ed. 1971
A Syllabus of Chinese Civilization, by J. Mason Gentzler, 2d ed. 1972
A Syllabus of Japanese Civilization, by H. Paul Varley, 2d ed. 1972
An Introduction to Chinese Civilization, ed. John Meskill, with the assistance of J. Mason Gentzler 1973
An Introduction to Japanese Civilization, ed. Arthur E. Tiedemann 1974
Ukifune: Love in the Tale of Genji, ed. Andrew Pekarik 1982
The Pleasures of Japanese Literature, by Donald Keene 1988
A Guide to Oriental Classics, eds. Wm. Theodore de Bary and Ainslie T. Embree; 3d edition ed. Amy Vladeck Heinrich, 2 vols. 1989

INTRODUCTION TO ASIAN CIVILIZATIONS

Wm. Theodore de Bary, General Editor

Sources of Japanese Tradition, 1958; paperback ed., 2 vols., 1964. 2d ed., vol. 1, 2001, compiled by Wm. Theodore de Bary, Donald Keene, George Tanabe, and Paul Varley
Sources of Indian Tradition, 1958; paperback ed., 2 vols., 1964. 2d ed., 2 vols., 1988
Sources of Chinese Tradition, 1960, paperback ed., 2 vols., 1964. 2d ed., vol. 1, 1999, compiled by Wm. Theodore de Bary and Irene Bloom; vol. 2, 2000, compiled by Wm. Theodore de Bary and Richard Lufrano

Sources of Korean Tradition, 1997; 2 vols., vol. 1, 1997, compiled by Peter H. Lee and Wm. Theodore de Bary; vol. 2, 2001, compiled by Yăngho Ch'oe, Peter H. Lee, and Wm. Theodore de Bary

NEO-CONFUCIAN STUDIES

Instructions for Practical Living and Other Neo-Confucian Writings by Wang Yang-ming, tr. Wing-tsit Chan 1963

Reflections on Things at Hand: The Neo-Confucian Anthology, comp. Chu Hsi and Lü Tsu-ch'ien, tr. Wing-tsit Chan 1967

Self and Society in Ming Thought, by Wm. Theodore de Bary and the Conference on Ming Thought. Also in paperback ed. 1970

The Unfolding of Neo-Confucianism, by Wm. Theodore de Bary and the Conference on Seventeenth-Century Chinese Thought. Also in paperback ed. 1975

Principle and Practicality: Essays in Neo-Confucianism and Practical Learning, eds. Wm. Theodore de Bary and Irene Bloom. Also in paperback ed. 1979

The Syncretic Religion of Lin Chao-en, by Judith A. Berling 1980

The Renewal of Buddhism in China: Chu-hung and the Late Ming Synthesis, by Chün-fang Yü 1981

Neo-Confucian Orthodoxy and the Learning of the Mind-and-Heart, by Wm. Theodore de Bary 1981

Yüan Thought: Chinese Thought and Religion Under the Mongols, eds. Hok-lam Chan and Wm. Theodore de Bary 1982

The Liberal Tradition in China, by Wm. Theodore de Bary 1983

The Development and Decline of Chinese Cosmology, by John B. Henderson 1984

The Rise of Neo-Confucianism in Korea, by Wm. Theodore de Bary and JaHyun Kim Haboush 1985

Chiao Hung and the Restructuring of Neo-Confucianism in Late Ming, by Edward T. Ch'ien 1985

Neo-Confucian Terms Explained: Pei-hsi tzu-i, by Ch'en Ch'un, ed. and trans. Wing-tsit Chan 1986

Knowledge Painfully Acquired: K'un-chih chi, by Lo Ch'in-shun, ed. and trans. Irene Bloom 1987

To Become a Sage: The Ten Diagrams on Sage Learning, by Yi T'oegye, ed. and trans. Michael C. Kalton 1988

The Message of the Mind in Neo-Confucian Thought, by Wm. Theodore de Bary 1989